Heard But Not Seen

By Daniel Morganstern

ISBN: 149604942X
ISBN-13: 978-1496049421

CONTENTS

ACKNOWLEDGMENTS

I would like to thank my wife, June DeForest Morganstern, for making my life possible, and to Elaine Fine, for making this book possible.

I thank John Ryden for his invaluable advice.

I thank Eliza Bangert for her tireless typing and proofreading of the manuscript, and dealing with the pre-publication process.

The cover was designed by Erin Kanary.

When Spencer Tracy talked about the role he played in "Judgment at Nuremberg," he referred to the lines he was able to speak as being the greatest privilege of his life. During my career I feel that I was immensely privileged to play 40 years of cello solos with the greatest ballet dancers and opera singers of the time, and to spend most of my days and nights intimately connected with some of the greatest music ever written.

INTRODUCTION

I distinctly remember being around three years old and drifting off to sleep to the sound of my mother playing the slow movement of the Chopin E Minor Piano Concerto. My mother graduated from high school at the age of 15, received a Bachelor's Degree from the Juilliard School of Music at the age of 18, and got her Master's Degree from Columbia University at 21. She was a brilliant and extraordinarily talented woman. Leonard Rose told me that he had many students who had mothers who played the piano, but that my mother was the only real artist among them.

My mother always wanted to learn to play the cello well enough to be able to play the second cello part in the Schubert C Major Quintet. She didn't realize, of course, that in order to play the second cello part you had to have real mastery of the instrument. Nevertheless, she bought a cello and tried to learn how to play it. When I was seven, it was time for me to learn an instrument. I wanted to play the violin, but my mother put a cello in my hands.

Dyslexia was a term first used in 1887 to describe a condition that makes reading difficult for people of otherwise normal intelligence. It is a condition that causes some people to unconsciously rotate two-dimensional images so that they become three-dimensional images. It is advantageous for sculptors and engineers, but before the condition was truly understood, it caused a great deal of strife for children who were learning to read.

I had a very poor self-image as a child because of my inability to read. One month into my fourth grade year, Mrs. Abigail Apt, my fourth grade teacher, had me stand up in front of the class. She told me that I had been on trial during the first month in order to see whether I could keep up with the class, and that I wasn't able to keep up. I felt my heart go straight down to my feet. Then she told me that everybody deserves a second chance, and announced that she would give me another month. She added that during this next month everybody in the class would help me. It must have worked, because I was able to complete the fourth grade.

My fifth grade teacher, Mrs. Fagin, was an ardent Republican who railed against Harry Truman for firing General MacArthur. Our class presented a program to honor fallen soldiers. People wrote stories and songs, and my mother and I played the first movement of Ludwig Mendelssohn's Cello Concerto. I had the honor of playing my older cousin Michael's cello for the occasion. After we played Mrs. Fagin came up to me and told me that nobody who can play the cello like that could possibly be dumb. Her statement rang in my mind, and it helped upgrade my self-image and my schoolwork significantly.

When I was eleven my aunt Lilly Grebanier (my mother's sister) encouraged my mother to send me to Carl Ziegler, my cousin Michael's teacher, for lessons. I idolized Michael and hoped that one day I could play as well as he played. His footsteps were hard to follow: when he was 19 Michael won the Naumberg Competition. He spent four years with George Szell in the Cleveland Orchestra as assistant principal, and then at age 25 was appointed principal cellist of the Pittsburgh Symphony.

Carl Ziegler was a member of the NBC Symphony under Arturo Toscanini, and a member of the New York City Ballet orchestra. He gave me pieces and etudes that were just a little harder than what I could do, and I managed to advance slowly. I learned the pieces he gave me, but I didn't make any earth-shaking progress.

I remember one lesson when I was playing the Boccherini Concerto for him while watching myself in the mirror. Mr. Ziegler laced into me and said, "I see that you're admiring yourself in the mirror." He continued, "If you listen to what you're doing, maybe you would find a lot less to admire, because at the rate you're going, you will never amount to anything as a cellist."

That comment shocked me out of my complacency, and I went home and I practiced for four hours. Why four hours? Because it had been widely reported to me that my cousin Michael practiced four hours a day. (Something he denies.) The next day I practiced for another four hours, and the day after that another four hours. I was a four-hour-a-day man. My playing improved dramatically, and Mr. Ziegler gave me much more difficult repertoire to learn. In a very short time, he helped me get through the Saint-Saëns Concerto and Lalo Concerto, as well as some difficult etudes by Piatti and Duport. He decided to give me one extra free lesson a week to cover the material he assigned, because, as he said, "It's good advertising for me." The next school year I was appointed the principal cellist of the All-City High School Orchestra, and I started developing a reputation as a really good cellist.

My mother was pleased with my progress, so she took it upon herself to contact Leonard Rose, who had heard me play in a little competition put on by WQXR. Maybe it wasn't so little, because the roster of judges included, at one time or another, Arthur Rubinstein, Zino Francescatti, Rudolph Serkin, Jascha Heifetz, and Leonard Rose. I did not win the prize, so my mother wrote to Leonard Rose to ask why. He replied, explaining that for my level I was the best around, and that it would do me a lot of good to find myself among other young cellists so that I could aspire to a higher level. He also said that it wouldn't hurt me to have a really first-class teacher (like him).

I was not happy to be carted off to Juilliard and away from Mr. Ziegler, whom I loved. I always understood that I would study with Leonard Rose *after* I graduated from high school, but my mother didn't give me a choice in the matter.

Mr. Rose spent the first lesson showing me how to sit properly at the cello and how to hold the bow. Before that lesson I had no idea how to sit properly or hold the bow in an efficient manner. I also had no idea how important it was.

One week after my first lesson with him, Mr. Rose gave a recital at Washington Irving High School. He played the Beethoven D Major Sonata, the Bach C Major Suite, and the Tchaikovsky "Rococo" Variations. He performed with such technical perfection, beauty of sound, and emotional warmth, that hearing that recital became the turning point of my life as a cellist. Being able to play like Leonard Rose became my only worthwhile goal.

My mother was right. Good things began to happen for me within my first few months of studying with Mr. Rose. A cello solo I played during the All-City High School Orchestra's Carnegie Hall concert was mentioned in the newspaper, and I won the WQXR "Musical Talent in Our Schools" contest. I also won the Brooklyn Philharmonic's first string competition, and made my debut as a soloist with the Brooklyn Philharmonic playing the Boccherini Concerto.

I was featured a large number of times on an educational television program called *Tune-up Time*. The main segments of the program were "blowing," "bowing," and "beating," and I was the star of the "bowing" part. In 1957 and 1958, when television was someplace between its infancy and adolescence, we had to wear blue shirts because white shirts reflected the light into the cameras in an unflattering way. I missed so many days of school that my history teacher tried to prevent me from graduating. When my picture appeared with Van Cliburn in the centerfold of the *Daily News* during his ticker-tape parade after winning the Tchaikovsky competition, my principal thwarted my history teacher's efforts. I also got a score of 89 on the Regents Exam and was legally prevented from failing by the state of New York.

Everything was going swimmingly, but I had a fall from grace when I played Faure's *Après un Reve* and the first movement of the Brahms E Minor Sonata on "Musical Talent in Our Schools." I was not unhappy with the way I played, and Abram Chasins (the director of the program) was ecstatic over my performance. Unfortunately Leonard Rose, who had heard the program, hated it. He read me the "riot act" in my next lesson, and all I could say in my defense was that I had listened to the acetate and thought it was pretty good. I still find it ironic that eighteen years later I got back into Leonard Rose's good graces as the anonymous cellist playing the solo in the second act of the national broadcast of *Swan Lake*. Who can tell the twists and turns of fate?

My first year as a college student at Juilliard came on the heels of all this success. My very first class there was ear training, and my teacher was the redoubtable Peter Schickele, a composer who achieved fame and fortune by creating the pseudo-18th-century character of P.D.Q. Bach. He used to give two-part dictation by burping the bass-line and whistling the melody. The class was filled with extraordinary people: some of them even became world-famous.

Leo Brouwer, my first friend in my ear-training class, was a composition major and a guitarist. When I asked him whether he played the piano, he told me that the guitar was his instrument, and that he composed on the guitar. He and his wife were most adamant about the fact that they were Cubans and not Puerto Ricans, and they often came visit me in Brooklyn where my mother was happy to feed them.

Leo and I played a recital together as a benefit for the Natalie Joan Chancy Foundation. I was impressed with the way he would strum his guitar until he was comfortable, and then launch into whatever it was he was going to play. He had a great career as a guitar virtuoso (his manager was Sol Hurok), and Leo became the most important and best-known composer in Cuba. He wrote for other instruments, but he is best known for his guitar music.

The soprano Shirley Verrett Carter (known professionally as Shirley Verrett) was fantastic when she came to sing at the Lyric Opera, but I will never forget the way she used to look over my shoulder when we had tests in ear-training class.

4

I met Channing Robbins very soon after my first day (I was his first student at Juilliard). I wanted to impress him, so I played three of the most difficult Popper etudes. I thought I played them flawlessly, and was waiting for admiring approval. All Channing said was, "You played an E-natural instead of an E-flat in one place." 17 years later, when I went back to work with him, I mentioned that since I had played so well he should have said something nice. He replied, "I would have known better now."

My inability to sight-read Strauss' *Don Juan* (or anything else, for that matter) prevented me from getting into the top orchestra at Juilliard. Fortunately there was a second orchestra, and its conductor, Jorge Mester, was delighted to have a principal cellist who already knew the solos from Rossini's *William Tell* Overture, Von Suppe's *Poet and Peasant* Overture, and Lalo's Le *Roi D'ys* Overture. He was an exceptional conductor, the first exceptional conductor I ever worked with. Sometimes he would comment on my interpretations, and I would say, "You do it your way and I'll do it Rossini's way." I worked with him 32 years later when I was the principal cellist of the Aspen Festival Orchestra. After playing under some of the best conductors in the world, I still found him exceptional.

Another conductor I met at Juilliard was Stefan Bauer Mengelberg, the grand nephew of the famous Willem Mengelberg. He was an assistant to Leonard Bernstein at the New York Philharmonic, and also taught mathematics at City College. Stefan arranged reading sessions of the Dvořák Concerto and the Barber Concerto so I could have a chance to play those pieces with orchestra (he went down to Schirmer's himself to get the orchestra parts for the Barber). When the weather was nice we would go to Riverside Park, and he would teach me advanced algebra.

One of the things that he told me he loved to spring on his classes had to do with sequences. I particularly remember his question about the relationship between 4, 14, 34, 42, and 59. It gave all of his students (including me) a headache to figure out. Finally he gave me the solution: those numbers are the station stops on the D train. He went to a lot of trouble for me. He got me tickets to performances of the New York Philharmonic and would treat me to dinner afterward at the Carnegie Deli.

After his incarnations as conductor and mathematician, he became a lawyer specializing in arts-related matters. He also invented a computer program to notate music. He sent me a very nice note before I played in Alice Tully Hall. He wished me luck and asked me if I wanted him to return my piano part for the Beethoven Sonatas. He expressed his regrets for not being able to come to the concert. I never saw him again.

The two summers that I spent at Meadowmount in 1957 and 1958 were crucial to my professional success. The atmosphere at Meadowmount was the total opposite the competitive atmosphere of Juilliard (a place where my colleagues were always ready to denigrate whatever accomplishments I may have had). At Meadowmount everyone was there to work in order to improve the way we played so we could advance in the profession. The atmosphere was totally positive, and I considered myself headed for success simply by being at Meadowmount.

I had interactions during those two summers with Ivan Galamian, Josef Gingold, and my own teacher, Leonard Rose. Leonard Rose pushed me to play more beautifully and with as much personality as possible. When I played the slow movement of the Dvořák Concerto for him, he told me, "If it don't got that swing, it don't mean a thing." Sometimes he would say, "Sock it to me, baby." The advanced students, like Roger Drinkall, were also willing to share both their knowledge of the repertoire and their knowledge about Mr. Rose's ways of teaching with younger students like me. Roger, who was a very fine cellist, spent a great deal of time helping me with the Dvořák Concerto and the Tchaikovsky "Rococo" Variations.

Mr. Rose asked Ivan Galamian to help me with my bow arm. After one of our fifteen-minute 6:45 a.m. lessons, Mr. Galamian took me to breakfast and talked to me about his philosophy of playing and teaching. We sat together beneath a placard that had a quote from Seneca that read "Most powerful is he who has himself in his own power." He told me, "It is easy to be easy on yourself and hard on the others, and it is hard to be hard on yourself and easy on the others, but much better." He also reminded me that while I may be talented, talent is not enough. Only hard work can bring it to fulfillment. It was certainly empowering that the most renowned violin teacher in the world was willing to spend his time trying to fix up my bow arm. It did wonders for my confidence.

In addition to the attention I got from Mr. Rose and Mr. Galamian, I had the opportunity to work through Franz Schubert's two-cello quintet with Joseph Gingold. Whatever he had to say about the way we played was much less important than his obvious love for the music, particularly his desire for it to be played as beautifully as possible.

Isaac Stern came and gave two very long masterclasses in 1957. The first class covered the Brahms Violin Sonatas, and the second covered the Bach Sonatas and Partitas. I was most impressed with how passionately interested he was in conveying his thoughts and feelings about these works. His way of teaching reminded me of the way Leonard Rose taught the cello repertoire, and I thought Mr. Stern was as fine a teacher as he was a player. Isaac Stern was 37 at the time and his career in full swing. It was very generous for him come to Meadowmount to work with students (though they were very good students: Jamie Laredo, Jerry Rosen, and Arnold Steinhardt).

I really enjoyed hearing the students at Meadowmount. Roger Drinkall gave a great performance of the Schubert "Arpeggione" Sonata, and I'm sure some of the panache he displayed then inspired my interpretation of the piece. Michael Grebanier, my cousin, performed the Brahms F Major Sonata and the Tchaikovsky "Rococo" Variations, which were part of his Naumberg recital program. Varoujon Kodjian gave a magnificent performance of the Khachaturian Violin Concerto, a piece I heard for the first time that summer, and Jamie Laredo gave a totally heartfelt rendition of the Sibelius Concerto. I also remember hearing Arnold Steinhardt practice Prokofieff's Second Concerto for hours on end.

I made great and lasting friendships at Meadowmount. Charles Haupt asked me to join his string quartet, and I had the opportunity to play through quartets of Schubert, Schumann, Ravel, and Debussy with extraordinary players. We remained good friends, and his wonderful violin playing inspired me throughout my career. I had the very good fortune to live with Paul Rosenthal, another violinist I met at Meadowmount, during the year that he was practicing for the Queen Elizabeth competition. His example showed me how to work on and maintain my own technique, and also how to achieve consistency at a very high level of playing. I owe much of my professional success to the associations and experiences I had at Meadowmount, as well as those I had during the summers I spent at Blue Hill in Maine.

Blue Hill was a summer music school founded in 1902 by Franz Kneisel. After 1953 Kneisel's daughter Marianne ran the school. I was a student there during the summers of 1959 and 1960, and I had the opportunity to work on the Beethoven Quartet, Opus 59, No. 1 and the Schubert Quartettsatz with the great violinist Joseph Fuchs. I learned a great deal from him, particularly when he would take over the first violinist's part and show us how to play chamber music. Right after my graduation from Juilliard, Marianne Kneisel engaged me to be one of two professional cellists to spend the summer there. This particular summer, I had a discussion with Mr. Fuchs that changed the course of my life.

Mr. Fuchs was very famous for speaking his mind, and when I met him one afternoon in front of Taco's Restaurant, he asked me if I was going back to Juilliard the next year. I told him I was thinking about it. He told me, "Don't go back to Juilliard. It's a big waste of time. Go out into the world. Get a job. Make money. You'll do well."

I took him at his word, and got a job.

I. SEPARATE CHECKS

Right after I graduated from Juilliard I became the fourth of four cellists in Mantovani's touring orchestra. During the 1950s and early 60s many touring orchestras traveled from place to place by bus, and when two busloads of musicians descended on a small diner at a rest stop someplace in the middle of nowhere for a half-hour break, the one unfortunate waitress was always assaulted with requests for separate checks.

Annunzio Paolo Mantovani (1905-1980) was the son of Bismark Mantovani, Arturo Toscanini's concertmaster at La Scala, Milan. His family moved to England in 1912 when Bismark got a conducting position at Covent Garden, and Annunzio began playing the violin there at the age of 14. His made his professional debut as a member of a touring orchestra at 16, and he became the conductor of the Hotel Metropole orchestra at the age of 20. During the 1930s he organized the Tipica Orchestra, and after World War II he gave his accordion player Ronald Binge (who was also a theater organist and composer) the job of arranging for his new Mantovani Orchestra. Binge arranged "Charmaine" using "cascading strings," an orchestration technique he devised to give the illusion of the kind of reverberation you find in a cathedral (or a theater organ) creating what would thereafter be known as "The Mantovani Sound." In 1951 Binge's arrangement of "Charmaine" became a million-record-selling hit in America, and so did Mantovani.

Mantovani traveled in a Cadillac limousine, and his principal players traveled in their own bus. One of the principal players I remember was David McCullom, our concertmaster. In addition to being the father of the actor (and one time oboe player) David McCullom, he had been the leader of the Royal Philharmonic before becoming Mantovani's concertmaster. I also remember George Swift, the principal trumpet player, who spent his time between shows haunting local pawnshops looking for old trumpets to sell back in England after the tour was over. There was also a principal flutist from Wales.

The rest of the touring orchestra traveled on a Greyhound-style bus with a sign in the front that read,

"HE MIGHT NOT ALWAYS BE RIGHT, BUT HE'S ALWAYS BOSS."

There were three different sorts of people on that bus. There were neophytes like me, middle-aged alcoholics who would drink 151-proof rum for breakfast, and senior citizens who could barely hold up their instruments. We played for Class B scale ($173 and change per week before taxes), out of which we had to pay our own hotel bills.

I had a few memorable encounters with the boss during this tour. After the first rehearsal I asked Mantovani and his librarian if I could take the music home to practice, and he remarked, "It says a lot about a person who takes his job seriously enough to want to practice the part." I was apparently the first person in the long history of the Mantovani Orchestra ever to make such a request. Our repertoire consisted of movie music like themes from *Lawrence of Arabia* and *Oliver!*, and gems that included the Brahms Hungarian Dance #5 (accompanying our concertmaster), Offenbach's "Can Can," "Moon River," "Old Folks at Home," and "Beautiful Dreamer." I knew that I was going to play this material 63 times during the nine-week tour, and did not expect to have much time to practice since the bus rides from city to city were six to eight hours long, so my actual reason for wanting the "book," as it was called, was to organize everything that I had to play into technical exercises so that I could maintain my playing skills while on tour.

Once, during a rehearsal of the "Can Can," I was doing my very best to play a series of descending scales as loudly as possible, so I did it with the requisite small amount of bow. Mantovani stopped the orchestra and said, "Young man! Please use the whole bow, frog to tip." I said, "But Maestro, it's a lot louder the way I'm doing it," to which he replied, "I don't care how it sounds. I care how it looks." There are times when I have used Mantovani's concept to great advantage.

My last personal encounter with Mantovani happened somewhere in the middle of Iowa. I was backstage practicing the third movement of the Kodály Solo Sonata, when Mantovani came over to me and said, "Young man, if only you realized that if you play with a beautiful sound, perfect intonation, and elegant phrasing, you wouldn't have to play music like that."

One of the younger violinists in the orchestra was David Frankl, a graduate of the Paris Conservatory. He, unlike our older alcoholic colleagues, particularly our concertmaster, who accused me of having fingers of steel and brains to match, appreciated my Kodály, as well as the fact that I practiced virtuoso etudes whenever it was possible to do so. When I finally developed the ability to exhibit the three qualities mentioned to me by Mantovani, however, I spent most of my time playing music by Schubert, Beethoven, and Brahms.

After each of the 63 performances that we gave, Mantovani would speak to the audience. He always said, "To play for an audience this appreciative has made our trip of 10,000 miles a privilege and a pleasure." We followed this little speech with an encore of *Charmaine*, which was always followed by thunderous applause and many curtain calls.

We always tried to save money since we made so little. In order to avoid spending money eating in restaurants, one of my colleagues lived on "Livermush," a concoction of liver and I don't know what else. During our bus rides, my colleagues and I would be in stitches taunting our penny-pinching associate by singing the tune of "Moon River" (one of the pieces in our repertoire) with the words, "Mush liver."

We had to pay for our own accommodations, so we developed ways to save money on hotel bills. We called one method "Ghosting." It involved one person registering for a room, and three people sleeping in it. The other method was "flea-bagging." We were always booked into first-class hotels, which would cost $5 or so per night, so many of us would scour the towns looking for $3 hotels. They were usually dilapidated and had bedbugs, but we were young and didn't care, as long as we could save those few extra dollars.

I spent many of the seemingly endless hours on the bus talking with my stand partner Richard Serbagi and Barrie Stott, a brilliant violinist who was a terribly disturbed human being. Serbagi and I were always looking out for him, and tried to keep him out of trouble (or jail), which proved to be an almost impossible task. When, for example, we were in Pensacola, Florida, Barrie insisted on going to the dock to try to pick up a sailor, and returned to the tour bus bloody and bruised. He engaged in other extremely risky behavior like driving on the Los Angeles freeway while drinking from a bottle of Jack Daniels. Ultimately, either by accident or by incident, he ended up killing himself.

Like the Brothers Karamazov there were four Serbagi brothers. Richard was the second. Midhat Serabgi was a violist who played in the Metropolitan Opera Orchestra. When he played a recital at Carnegie

Recital Hall he wore a red suit, and sang the role of the viola-playing Turk from John Corigliano's *Ghosts of Versailles*. Roger Serabgi became a fairly well-known actor and appeared often on television shows like *Law and Order* and *Spencer for Hire*. When Mantovani played in Boston, I met Russell, the fourth brother, who didn't do much of anything musical. I believe that I am one of the few people who knew Richard Serbagi who ever met this particular brother.

The Mantovani tour had a concert in Pittsburgh, the home of my fiancee June's parents, and Serbagi insisted that I get some decent clothes before meeting them for the first time. I didn't own any decent clothes up to that point because I never had any money. We had a few days off between Baltimore and Pittsburgh, so Serbagi took me to a clothing store and made sure I bought a nice jacket, a tweedy overcoat, several shirts and a few bow ties. Serbagi took my cello on the Mantovani bus, I took a bus from Baltimore to Pittsburgh, and we made arrangements for June and her parents to pick me up at the bus stop in Pittsburgh. I imagine that it was because of my sartorial splendor that June's father took a real liking to me. Serbagi was sort of like a big brother who gave me good advice about things that I didn't know.

Serbagi got me a job recording David Amram's Incidental Music to Molière's *Tartuffe*, a show that was playing at one of the theaters in Lincoln Center. One number was a difficult perpetual motion for cello. During the intervals when the cello wasn't needed, I put fingerings over every note. By reading the numbers, I was able to pull it off.

I had to figure out unusual solutions to musical problems because I never could sight read anything. When I was a child I learned music by having my mother play it for me on the piano, and I would very quickly pick it up by ear. When I played in orchestras, even good ones like the All-City High School Orchestra in New York, I would do what my stand partner was doing, and memorize it quickly. This was only a problem when I was sight reading music. I didn't have problems reading music that I already knew.

My method of compensating was to go through a section of music carefully, hear what it sounded like, and write fingerings over every note. Then the complete picture would come into my mind when I looked at again, and the music was already in a semi-memorized form. It was frustrating not to be able to actually *read* the notes in front of me and make any sense out of them, but once I did make sense out of them, I saw and heard a much wider band of music in my head than most of the people around me seemed to be able to see and hear.

I was able to play all of my recitals by memory, and only had one memory slip in my entire solo career (and it was a shock). After studying the Beethoven D Major Sonata for only three or four weeks, I was able to play the entire sonata including the fugue by memory at a video recording session (a distinct advantage for the camera shots).

Early in my career I was on tour with the Harkness Ballet playing Andre Jolivet's *Ariadne,* a piece that had a wicked cello solo. I had to learn it interval by interval. It was a tedious process, to be sure, but once I learned it, I never missed anything. I remember taking eight hours to figure out Schoenberg's *Verklärte Nacht* and thinking what an idiot I was and how disadvantaged I was to have to work so hard. Thirty years later I could still play most of it from memory. My time-honored technique for learning anything complicated was to put on the metronome at a very slow tempo, usually at 40 beats per minute, and play a small section until I knew how it went. It's that simple. Once I did know how something went, I could recall it instantly. I depended a great deal on having fingerings written over the notes in my music, something I could only get away with by being in the first chair of a section. I had a glorious career in the principal cello chair of a great ballet orchestra and a great opera orchestra, because that was the safest place for me to be.

II. FANCY FREE

My 35-year tenure at the American Ballet Theatre began on a Tuesday evening in early January 1964, when I got a call from Erik Kessler, the contractor and principal horn player for the American Ballet Theatre orchestra. It seemed that my colleague from the Mantovani orchestra, David Frankl, had recommended me to William Brohn, one of the American Ballet Theatre Orchestra's three conductors. Mr. Kessler urgently needed a principal cellist for a touring orchestra, and offered me $212 a week, a full ten dollars over Class A scale, if I would play. Since "principal cello" meant "only cello" in a skeleton orchestra of seventeen players, I asked him for $215. I guess he was desperate enough not to haggle over three dollars, so the deal was set.

The next morning I went to the American Ballet Theatre office at Broadway and 58th Street and picked up the cello music for the 17 ballets we would be playing. There were 15 hours of rehearsals scheduled for Thursday, Friday, and Saturday. After a long bus trip with a stop in Columbus, Ohio, the first performance would be on Tuesday in St. Louis.

I looked through the music casually, but when I came to Leonard Bernstein's *Fancy Free* I was so shocked by the complicated rhythms on the first three pages that I felt like I would have a heart attack. I wanted to go back to the office and tell Eric Kessler that he had made a terrible mistake, but I decided to go home first. I showed *Fancy Free* to my fiancée, and told her that it was beyond my ability to figure out the rhythms. I told her that the most sensible thing for me to do under the circumstances was to resign. June felt differently. She suggested that I should go to the first rehearsal and let them fire me (and this was before

Woody Allen reminded his readers and audiences that 80% of success comes from merely showing up).

All I could think of to do was to go down to Sam Goody, a well-stocked record store on 9th Avenue, and buy a recording of *Fancy Free*. I listened to it over and over until, at about 3:00 a.m., I knew the cello part well enough to sing it, so at 10:00 a.m. I showed up at Carroll Studios on 48th Street and 8th Avenue.

Our primary conductor was Walter Hagen. Before becoming a conductor he played second violin in the Gordon Quartet (the cellist of that quartet was Luigi Silva, one of my teachers), and was the principal second violinist of the Metropolitan Opera Orchestra. He actually began his conducting career in the Metropolitan Opera pit during a 1957 performance of *La Forza del Destino*. The conductor, Pietro Cimara, had a sudden stroke and started to slump. Walter stepped in to stop the conductor from falling, and then took his baton and conducted the opera until medical help came and a more experienced replacement could be found. The story made the front page of the *New York Times*, and Walter was very happy to make the switch from being a career second violinist to being a conductor.

At the beginning of the rehearsal Walter told the orchestra that we should bring a lot of books and games on the tour because we would have many long bus trips (this I understood). We began the rehearsal with Johann Strauss's *Graduation Ball* and the Chausson *Poème,* a piece I knew very well. We didn't hit the dreaded *Fancy Free* until the second day of rehearsal, and when we did I was surprised and delighted that all the difficult rhythms on the first three pages were unison passages. I was totally covered up and could happily play along by ear without any problem. There were other ballets that had other difficulties, and there were solos. I soberly accepted that it was my job to figure out how to safely execute anything I had to play, particularly if it was exposed, and was comforted by the knowledge that my colleagues had all been through this kind of trial by fire.

The St. Louis performance was in Powell Hall, and my solos in *Les Sylphides* and the Mendelssohn Piano Concerto went fine, but the performance a few days later in Lawton, Oklahoma was traumatic because Copland's *Billy the Kid* was on the program. *Billy the Kid* has a lot of tricky exposed cello entrances that happen to come on different beats, and playing by ear, my *modus operandi*, wasn't working very well. Bill Brohn was conducting, and he must have noticed the terror in my eyes because he threw every entrance at me while muttering under his breath, "Learn to count! Learn to count!"

I confessed my orchestral inadequacies to Walter Hagen, and I told him that I was particularly horrified about playing the 7/4 section of Ture

Rangström's *Miss Julie*. Walter's response was to sit with me on the bus during the next week and solfege the cello parts with me. He conducted while I sang, so I could coordinate everything with his stick. During the rest of this tour, which lasted for eight weeks, my confidence increased exponentially since there were no other ballets to learn than the 17 that I had started with. By the end of the third week I had pretty well memorized just about all of it and, as with the Mantovani tour, started practicing during the performances. Two things that stand out in my mind were that in the ensuing 35 years that I remained principal cellist of the American Ballet Theatre Orchestra, we never had a conducting staff equal to the one that accompanied this eight-week tour with the skeleton orchestra (Walter Hagen, William Brohn, and Kenneth Schermerhorn, who joined the tour late in the fourth week, because his wife Lupe Serrano, the prima ballerina of ABT, had just had a baby).

There was often little time to practice between performances on tour, so I got in the habit of using good exercises to warm up properly before playing. Since we repeated the same ballets, I could experiment using the very familiar material to improve my sound from performance to performance. Since I was the only cellist, I could try whatever outlandish solutions came to mind, even those that failed. I never got bored with trying to sound better, and I developed a lifelong habit of enthusiastically embracing whatever material I had to play, whenever I had to play it. I was consequently very well prepared to make an excellent impression when I found myself in the principal cello seat at the New York State Theater in 1965, particularly when I knew my older colleagues didn't expect much from a 24-year-old.

The most important thing I learned during this tour was how to make the cello part work with the entire orchestral score effectively without help from anybody, since there was nobody for me to get any help from. I believe that over my entire career, this mindset of making the cello part effectively empower an orchestral score and always maintaining my highest possible level of playing served me well.

III. SADIST OR SAINT

During my final year at Juilliard I had a cello student named David Fink (he later changed his name to Finch), who happened to be the stepson of Leonard Shure, a protégé of Artur Schnabel and one of the greatest pianists of the day. After my graduation Mr. Shure invited me to his home and asked me about my aspirations. I told him that my ambition was to acquire a technique that was so good and reliable that I would be able to play anything perfectly at any time. His response was, "I sincerely hope you never get your great technique." After I asked him why he responded, "If you get your great technique, you will always demean the music that you are playing down to the level of what you can easily do. On the other hand, if you look at a piece of music, particularly a great piece of music, on a note-by-note and phrase-by-phrase basis and continually ask yourself what the music demands, in finding a way to meet those demands your technique can become as infinite as the music." He then offered to teach me in exchange for my lessons with David, a lopsided arrangement, to say the least.

Mr. Shure was one of the greatest musicians I have ever known. His phrasing was so absolute that when you listened to him play you would find yourself breathing only where he let you breathe. Sadly, I only heard this level of artistry from him when he played in his living room. When he got on stage all spontaneity left him, and he became very didactic.

Since I was a cellist, not a pianist, I managed to avoid his technical criticism, but I did observe the sadistic way he treated his piano students. One in particular was a brilliant Israeli pianist with whom I played the Beethoven A Major Sonata in his class. I thought she was a wonderful pianist with a free and easy style that was characterized by buoyancy and effervescence. Mr. Shure constantly and unremittingly accused her of being a right-handed pianist, and brought her to tears week after week. After a year of this treatment, she left to go to Juilliard and study with Rosina Lhévinne. He would ask all the students, in his chamber music classes as well as in his piano classes, to follow the score assiduously, and everybody would point out whatever omissions or commissions offended the print. I never cared for this approach because I always felt that it wasn't what was in the score, per se, but what *wasn't* in the score that created real artistry.

I did learn a great deal from my lessons with Leonard Shure. Once I played the Gigue of the Second Bach Suite in a manner that was not awfully convincing. Mr. Shure played it on the piano with enough verve and panache to make me want to get up and start dancing. He then asked, "Do you know why I sound so good and you sound so bad?" to which I replied, "If I knew that, I probably wouldn't need to be here." He told me that it was because he sees the keyboard as a point of resistance, and always comes *from* the point of resistance. If you go *to* the point of resistance, as soon as you hit the note it's all over. If you come *from* the point of resistance, there's infinite variety that can be drawn out of the instrument.

The usual way of getting sound out of the cello is to press it out. This is an outside-in approach that forces tension and a promotes paint-by-number musical mindset. I think Mr. Shure's technical advice applies even *more* to playing a string instrument than it does to playing the piano because string instruments have two different points of resistance: the string under the fingers of the left hand and the string through the bow. If a cellist thinks of the act of drawing sound out of the instrument as a release, there's no limit to the variety of sound that can come out of the instrument without the cellist getting tight.

Mr. Shure had a particular attitude when he played the Beethoven Cello Sonatas with me. He didn't seem to think that the Beethoven A Major Cello Sonata was that different from any one of the middle-period piano sonatas; it just had an annoying cello part tagging along. From this attitude I started to see everything that I played as a complete, contextual picture. I learned to relate whatever I happened to be playing to the entire score.

When I asked Mr. Shure why he lavished so much time and attention on me, particularly since I wasn't paying him his usual $30-an-hour fee, he said, "I believe someday you will carry my work into the future."

Mr. Shure had high aspirations for my development, but he violently objected to the ways in which I earned a living. I could not afford to abandon all sources of income in favor of studying Beethoven, Brahms, and Schubert. I was obliged to go on ballet tours and accept other cello-playing work in order to pay the bills.

Two years into our relationship, he organized a recital in his home. He played Schubert's *Die Wintereise* with a singer on the first half of the concert, and Ursula Oppens and I played the Brahms F Major Sonata on the second half. Ursula and I decided that we would play a little joke on Mr. Shure, and asked if we could play an encore. He said, "By all means!" at which point we launched into the Popper *Hungarian Rhapsody*, full of tasteless slides and faster-than-the- speed-of-light spiccatos. When we finished (and I can still hear his voice) he said, "Some of you may think this is funny. I do not. Circuses do not belong in churches. You are known by your face. Who are you? Are you an artist playing the Brahms F Major, or a clown, wailing away in the most appalling bad taste? You are invited to leave and never come back." That was the end of my relationship with and Leonard Shure.

Twenty-odd years later I played a Beethoven cycle in Carnegie Recital Hall and got a wonderful review from a notably tough critic, Bernard Holland. I sent a copy to Leonard Shure; thanking him for everything he taught me, and assuring him that this performance would not have been possible without his teaching and influence. I received no reply.

My decision to continue touring with the American Ballet Theatre was a turning point in my early professional life, and I have the cello solos in *La Sylphide* and *Giselle* to thank for being offered the principal cello position for the 1965 New York season at the New York State Theatre.

As the principal cellist I was given the opportunity to choose my stand partner, so I chose Carl Ziegler, my first cello teacher. Mr. Ziegler was delighted when I asked him to be my stand partner. I told him about my problems with sight-reading and about how I learned the ballet repertoire by memory (I didn't understand at the time that my difficulties were due to dyslexia) to compensate for my lack of professionalism. Mr. Ziegler's response was, "What could be more professional than knowing the music you have to play by memory?"

Mr. Ziegler was a wonderful assistant, and he beamed with pleasure (and maybe a bit of pride) every time I played a solo.

IV. A NEW CELLO

After spending many years in relative obscurity in New York (and on bus tours everywhere else), by the early 1960s the American Ballet Theatre had become one of the primary ballet companies in the world. The 1965 Season for the American Ballet Theatre was a very important one. It was billed as the company's 25th anniversary, and it was the season that earned American Ballet Theatre the very first grant issued by the National Endowment for the Arts. The company began in 1937 under the name "Ballet Theatre" by Mikhail Mordkin, a former dancer with the Bolshoi Ballet, and his student Lucia Chase. A few years later Richard Pleasant, a one-time Hollywood agent, came to New York to work with Chase to turn the company into a "living museum of dance," offering an alternative to George Balanchine's single-choreographer approach. In 1956 the company changed its name to "American Ballet Theatre." Lucia Chase spent her entire career dancing in the company, directing the company, and backing it financially. When she retired in 1980, Mikhail Baryshnikov became the director.

1965 was the first season that the American Ballet Theatre performed in the newly built New York State Theater in the equally new collection of schools, libraries, theaters and concert halls known as Lincoln Center. The State Theater was designed, to the specifications of George Balanchine, by Philip Johnson and was built with funds from the State of New York as part of the 1964-1965 World's Fair.

The 1965 season included some important performances. Sallie Wilson, the leading expert on Anthony Tudor's ballets, danced in his *Dark Elegies* (set to Mahler's *Kindertotenlieder*) and *Lilac Garden* (set to the Chausson *Poème*). She and Elliot Feld rode on the bus with the musicians, and both of them knew a lot about music. Feld played the flute, and would often stay up all night gambling. We performed Agnes de Mille's *Wind in the Mountains*, with a score by Laurence Rosenthal. Agnes de Mille was married to Walter Prude, an extremely important person in the world of concert management (he managed Arthur Rubinstein, Marian Anderson, and Isaac Stern), and the dancers would sometimes refer to her as "Agony Prude." Another highlight of that season was the first American Ballet Theatre performance of Stravinsky's *Les Noces* with Leonard Bernstein conducting.

After that New York season, I began a fairly long tour with a ballet company created by Rebekah Harkness. Mrs. Harkness was one of the wealthiest women in America, and fancied herself a composer, sculptor, and a patron of the arts, particularly of ballet. Her wealth came from the countless shares of Standard Oil that she inherited from one of her many husbands.

Clive Barns described the Harkness Ballet as "perhaps a company of splendid dancers in search of a splendid ballet." Harkness seemed to think that she could achieve the results of George Balanchine if she could assemble a group of young composers, dancers, designers, and choreographers and give them a place to work (her home in Newport) and places to perform. She proved very publicly that all the money in the world, though it can pay salaries, cannot buy artistic success, and she will be remembered (if at all) mainly for her tantrums, excesses, and for the way she squandered her fortune. Craig Unger wrote about her life, failed marriages, and misadventures in his 1989 book *Blue Blood*.

The musicians traveled on a crowded bus, and Mrs. Harkness traveled in a chauffer-driven sky blue Rolls Royce. With the one exception of "Pas de deux" from Tchaikovsky's *Sleeping Beauty*, the repertoire was some of the worst music I ever heard, particularly *Yomanja,* Mrs. Harkness' own ballet that she based on Native American legends. We also performed a ballet set to a piece by Mrs. Harkness' composition teacher, Lee Hoiby.

Even a regular paycheck was not adequate compensation for what we had to put up with. It was with the greatest possible pleasure that I returned to New York and the 1966 American Ballet Theatre season at the State Theater.

I had an accident with my cello that year. A strong gust of March wind caught my cello case and sent it flying across Columbus Avenue, leaving me holding the handle. Miraculously the cello was not destroyed, but it was damaged. Since I needed a cello to finish the season, I borrowed one from Ava Bry, an old girlfriend. Her cello was something I used to call a "Joseph Settin special." It was an old cello in bad repair that sounded terrific, and could be had for a modest amount of money.

Since I had the means to get one of these for myself, I went to Settin's shop on West 57th Street in Manhattan. I tried out several instruments, but there was only one that really made my heart sing. The problem was that Mr. Settin had no intention of selling that cello. He was unwilling to tell me specifically why, but was adamant about the fact that this cello was not going to me or anyone else.

At that critical moment the very famous (in fact legendary) violinist Mischa Elman came into the shop. Elman was the first of Leopold Auer's students to make it big in the world, and he had the most beautiful tone of any violinist. The rise to fame of Jascha Heifetz really cramped his style, and he always felt unjustly overshadowed. There is a very famous story that at Heifetz's 1917 debut, Elman complained that it was awfully hot at Carnegie Hall, to which his companion replied, "Not for pianists." He was also a world-class neurotic who haunted the violin shops in New York, getting continuous adjustments to his Stradivarius; hence his appearance at that critical moment. I asked him to listen to this cello, and being a sucker for a beautiful sound, he loved the instrument. He then told me my name should not be Morganstern, which means "morning star," but Abendstern, which means "evening star." When I told Mr. Elman that Mr. Settin was not willing to sell this cello to me, he interceded on my behalf saying, "The boy deserves to have a beautiful instrument. Sell him the cello." And so, not being able to refuse Mischa Elman, the deal was struck and I went out with that cello.

At the time I knew that Mischa Elman was a very famous violinist, but I had never actually heard him play. During the next two years I attended recitals he gave at Carnegie Hall, and was astonished at the beauty and luminosity of his sound. Two performances particularly impressed me. In the Brahms G Major Sonata when the piano takes over the first theme and the violin accompanies, pizzicato, it sounded more like a harp than a violin. In the intricate bowings in the second movement of Beethoven's "Kreutzer" Sonata, his articulations had incredible clarity, even in the balcony where I was sitting. Perhaps if I had known the greatness of his playing, I might not have had the courage to ask him to listen to *me* play.

My new cello brought me luck. A few weeks later my violinist friend Jesse Ceci invited June and me to his apartment for dinner. I had to leave the dinner early because I had a performance with the Bolshoi Ballet at the old Metropolitan Opera House on 40th Street. This was one of the last performances given in that historic building before it was demolished. On the elevator ride down from Jesse's apartment I met two elegantly dressed neighbors of Jesse's who looked like they were going someplace like the ballet. I asked them if they were going to the Met that night. It turned out that they were, so we shared a cab. During the cab ride I told my new friend Henson Markham all about my new cello.

Henson Markham and his wife Julia invited me to come back with them after the performance so that I could show them my cello. Henson was an avid amateur musician and had a harpsichord in his apartment, so we got June and Jesse from Jesse's apartment and played some of the Brandenburg Concertos. Henson and I have remained friends for decades, and he has given me excellent advice throughout my career.

On June 12, 1966, I played my first New York recital. It was at the Brooklyn Museum. The pianist was Richard Goode, and Henson turned pages. Our program included the Bach G Minor Viola da Gamba Sonata, the Hindemith Unaccompanied Sonata, and the Brahms E Minor Cello Sonata. This recital, which was scheduled a week before my wedding, was broadcast over WNYC, and Richard gave me the gift of his services as a wedding present.

I first played with Richard in December of 1965 when Jesse Ceci asked me to play the Schumann G Minor Trio. Richard was only 22 at the time, but it was clear to me that he was a truly great artist. He did eventually become not only one of the greatest pianists of our age, but in my opinion, one of the greatest pianists of all ages. His recordings of the complete Beethoven piano sonatas, Schubert sonatas, and Bach partitas are peerless.

Shortly after we played the Schumann, I got a frantic call from Richard asking me if I would play with him at the home of Mrs. Leventritt. Mrs. Leventritt was a famous patron of the arts who ran a very important competition. I found Richard's request too intimidating to accept because I knew that every great musician of the time had played in her living room. I pleaded with him to try to find somebody else, but two hours later he called back and said he couldn't find anybody else, and he really needed me to do him that favor.

When I arrived at Mrs. Leventritt's Park Avenue apartment, Richard, Murray Perahia, Pinchas Zukerman, and Mrs. Leventritt were waiting for me. I was invited immediately to sit down and play the Brahms F Major Sonata with Richard. After that, Pinchas Zukerman joined us for the Schumann G Minor Trio. I will never forget my sense of futility trying to compete with the seventeen-year-old Zukerman. There was just nothing I could do to match his sound. After we finished, Richard and Murray Perahia played some Schubert four-hand duos, and then we all sat down for cookies and conversation.

Mrs. Leventritt showed me that my endpin had gone into the same hole in her floor that Feuermann's Strad had also been tethered when *he* played the Brahms F Major for her. We had a discussion about conductors. I remember her saying that all the great ones are real SOBs, and that it seems to be part of their talent. When I disagreed, saying that I had worked with some fine conductors who weren't SOBs, she assured me they were simply not in the class with George Szell, Fritz Reiner, and Arturo Toscanini. How could I argue with that? I still remember poignantly the cab ride from the East side to the West side where we all lived. In the back seat of a cab with my cello, Richard, and Pinky, I was assured that I had played well. In my opinion, they were being kind.

Richard Goode was the first of many remarkable musicians I worked with that summer. I was asked to be the principal cellist and chamber music coach for the fourth Congregation of the Arts at Dartmouth College, a position formerly held by Channing Robbins, who was a distinguished professor of cello at the Juilliard School of Music. This festival featured residencies by such famous composers as Kodály, Ginastera, and Lutoslawski, and had an absolutely first class faculty. The violinists included David Cerone, who became the long time president of the Cleveland Institute; William Steck, who ultimately became concertmaster of the National Symphony; and Stuart Canin, the first American to win the Paganini Competition, and who became the concertmaster of the San Francisco Symphony. Other musicians included Paul Olefsky, the former principal cellist of both the Philadelphia Orchestra and the Detroit Symphony; and Alfred Genovese, the former principal oboe of the Metropolitan Opera, and later of the Boston Symphony. I was able to survive playing eight orchestral concerts of predominantly contemporary music, and hold my own with my vastly more experienced colleagues.

I had a memorable encounter at Dartmouth with Witold Lutoslawski. We were working on his Concerto for Orchestra, a piece I admired a great deal, so since he was such a superb composer, I asked him if he would help me analyze Franz Schubert's C Major Quintet. My request was heartfelt, and he just happened to have the cello constantly on his mind since he was at work composing his Cello Concerto. He generously spent several hours with me, and he treated me with respect that I don't think I really deserved. As with Mischa Elman, if I had known how great his stature actually was, I would not have had the courage to ask.

When I returned to New York I learned that my friend Walter Hagen, the principal conductor of the American Ballet Theatre, was fired for the simple reason that Lucia Chase, the founder and general director of the company, decided that she preferred someone else. This decision had nothing to do with Walter's ability as a conductor. June and I felt a great deal of loyalty to Walter since he was the person who hired both of us, so we quit. Fortunately for us, Walter was immediately hired as Principal Conductor for the competing Joffrey Ballet, where June and I found employment as concertmaster and principal cellist.

During the Joffrey Ballet tour I was working up the "Rococo" Variations for a recital at the Lincoln Center Library. Every time I practiced the piece, Gerald Arpino, the famous choreographer, came around to listen. Eventually he choreographed a ballet to it, but someone else got to play the premiere since I was on tour with the American Ballet Theatre, which I rejoined after Walter was safely ensconced at Joffrey.

It occurred to me that if a conductor of Walter's ability could be fired for no good reason, I could suffer the same fate very easily, and so I created one of my life laws: if they *can* screw you they *will* screw you. This does not necessarily mean that you will get screwed right away. It means that if circumstances change, a person can become vulnerable. In order to counteract this possibility I decided that there were only two possible courses of action. The first course of action is to get them to not want to screw you by constantly exhibiting a level of ability and accomplishment well above either the requirements of the job and/or the other colleagues, and at the same time be supportive and pleasing, even ingratiating, to those people who have the power to hire and fire. The second course of action would be to legally prevent them from firing me, if this were possible. Eventually I joined forces with other colleagues to create the American Ballet Theatre Orchestra Committee with the backing of Local 802 of the American Federation of Musicians, and accomplished just that.

V. THE DIVINITY THAT SHAPES OUR ENDS

In 1967 I auditioned for a seventeen-week-long American tour of the Royal Ballet, which featured Rudolf Nureyev and Margot Fonteyn. Max Gershunoff, who knew my playing from the previous American Ballet Theatre season, considered it an audition for assistant principal to Albert Catell, who had been the principal cellist for Hurok Attractions for years. He also hired June for the violin section.

Albert Catell studied with both Emanuel Feuermann and Julius Klengel, and was a true representative of that great school of cello playing (something he never let me forget). He was very reliable and had a beautiful sound, but he played somewhat out of tune. He used to chide me for practicing so much, saying things like, "He who practices needs it," and various other denigrations whenever opportunity presented itself (which was often). I feel fortunate that I was able to see and hear an experienced and excellent cellist play the many important solos in the ballet repertoire.

The tour began with a six-week run at the Metropolitan Opera House and then we traveled to San Francisco, Los Angeles, Seattle, Vancouver, Toronto, Chicago, Boston, and Philadelphia. We traveled by airplane, and stayed in each city for at least a week, a serious improvement over the conditions on previous tours. June bought her 1706 Grancino violin during our week in San Francisco, and has played that instrument throughout her entire career.

We brought four of the greatest full-length ballets ever written on tour: Prokofiev's *Romeo and Juliet* and *Cinderella*, and Tchaikovsky's *Sleeping Beauty* and *Swan Lake*, and played under the quintessential

English conductor John Lanchbery. Known as "Jack" to his friends, he was one of the finest conductors I ever worked with.

Jack was 43 years old and in his prime. He was an accomplished composer and arranger, which contributed to his outstanding interpretations of these works. He would reinterpret the works he was conducting in order to favor the strengths of the orchestra's best players. He had a huge vocabulary and wonderful way with words like "mellifluous," "expunge," and "fecund." He also had a fantastic sense of humor. I can't resist at this point including one of his jokes.

Medical students at Oxford decided to give the very famous lady theologian a hard time. One of them said, "Madame, how DO you reconcile the fact that God made man in his own image with the Jewish rite of circumcision?" She replied, "That's an easy one. Shakespeare said it best when he said, 'There is a divinity which shapes our ends, rough-hewn them as we will.'"

When he wanted more bite out of the cello section, Jack would say, "Let's have some toast for the poached eggs." He could empower a player to play beyond his or her normal capacities. I was totally terrified of him, but we became very good friends, and we often had breakfast together when we were on the road.

Later, when Jack became music director of the American Ballet Theatre and I was the principal cellist, he inserted cello solos into his arrangements, saying that I was irresistible in the key of D minor. I played solos with him in performances of *Giselle*, *Bayadere*, and *Sleeping Beauty*, which were broadcast on the "Live from Lincoln Center" PBS series, and played countless performances of *Swan Lake* and other popular ballets that were not televised. My greatest experience with Jack was doing several performances of Schoenberg's *Pierrot Lunaire* at the Met, with Rudolf Nureyev dancing the role of Pierrot. Working with Jack taught me to have confidence in my ability to please conductors, particularly the excellent conductors I would later encounter at the Lyric Opera of Chicago. A treasured autographed picture of Jack hangs in my studio.

Three young people used to show up at every single performance on our 1967 Royal Ballet Tour. They would travel (perhaps hitchhike) from one city to the next. One young lady named Helene was obviously in love with Rudolph Nureyev, and she pestered him to the point where he finally hit her. It incensed me so much that when Nureyev took his bow I would boo him. Nureyev tried to get me fired for this, but Jack told him that it was not possible. Jack suggested that I should look the other way.

Rudy was a real artist. Helene, a true balletomane, compared him to Michael Baryshnikov when Baryshnikov came to the American Ballet Theatre in 1974, and considered Baryshnikov a mere acrobat compared to Rudy. Nureyev came to the American Ballet Theatre as a conductor near the end of his losing battle with AIDS. It was his lifelong desire to conduct Prokofiev's *Romeo and Juliet*. I took off the run, but my colleagues told me he did well. I was faced in the opposite direction when I worked with him, so his artistry was totally lost on me.

VI. GERALD BEAL TO THE RESCUE

Gerald Beal had been a famous child prodigy who toured the world under Columbia Artists Management with his identical twin brother Wilfred, playing the Bach Double Concerto and other works for two violins. Jerry had a tendency to make things up, so I tried to stay out of his way during the tour, but one day between matinee and an evening performance at the Metropolitan Opera House, I heard him play an extraordinary performance of the Bach C Major Fugue.

Jerry was a long-time student of Ivan Galamian, and he had also studied privately with Jascha Heifetz. Because of this, my wife asked him to give her a lesson on how to practice scales. I was interested as well, so I listened to the lesson, and then I asked Jerry to show me a few things. I was so impressed with what he taught me that I spent the rest of the tour and the next five years studying with him.

It is said when the student is ready, the teacher appears. This was absolutely true for me at that time. I was playing well, but I was doing so with a great amount of physical tension. The first thing that Beal did was to give me a series of very clever exercises to re-sensitize me to the cello. The object was often to see how little pressure was required in either hand to create a sound, and to work up from there. Beal taught me to listen to myself. He would have me play through slow movements, making sure I would vibrate on every note. If I happened to play a single note without vibrato, I would have to start again at the beginning. I felt like Sisyphus.

Beal reduced technique down to a few basic elements, and could organize the execution of any melody or passage around a few simple principles. He reminded me that every note has a beginning, which is an attack of some sort; a middle, which is a development of the sound; and an end, which is either a tapering off or a connection to another note. He had me practice this by playing scales and arpeggios, one note to a bow, in order to develop a complete command of balance and vibrato. To Beal, the trick was to create the greatest amount of beauty on the longest note of a phrase, and organize the rest of the notes in a particular phrase around it.

He taught me about the way silence connects to sound, the infinite variety of sound once created, and how that sound could join either to silence or to another sound. Jerry taught me to organize my playing in terms of attack and release, and after I learned to manage the release part, I found I had a great deal of control.

Jerry worked tirelessly with me when I had important solos to play (before my first rehearsal at the Lyric Opera, he took me through the entire cello part of *Salome*. It took eight hours a day for three days to get through it all, but in the end I could play it like a concerto, and lots of it by memory). He understood the importance of making a stunning and permanent impression, and over the next five years he gave me as many lessons as he thought I needed, covering solo and chamber music repertoire as well as orchestral solos. Jerry knew that he had an unsavory reputation, which may be the reason he encouraged me not to mention him as one of my teachers. He assured me that the name of Leonard Rose would carry a great deal more weight, and would cast me in a more positive light.

Jerry pounded his concept of rhythm into me, hour after hour, at every lesson. He would sing and conduct and click out rhythmic subdivisions while I played in order to create a framework for attacking and releasing. He taught me that as long as the interval between pulses is predictable, anything done in between pulses would be plausible. He taught me that the challenge is to keep the pulses as far apart as possible. If I take a melody and pulse it by the quarter note, and then I pulse the same melody (in the same tempo) by the half note, by the measure, by two measures, by four measures, or by eight measures, each statement of the melody would be correct, but the amount of freedom offered by the longer interval between pulses makes it possible to bring *imagination* to bear.

I was always told that you should never make a musical virtue out of a technical vice, and that you should work out your problems. When I proposed this notion to Jerry Beal, he would laugh in my face, and say, "If at first you don't succeed, try something else." For Jerry, any plausible way of organizing a group of notes was perfectly good, so picking one that featured your strengths, rather than your weaknesses, seemed the obvious choice. Comfort and security were more important to Jerry than conjuring up the most transcendental phrase imaginable.

Jerry Beal taught me that every phrase must make a point that cannot be missed. The best non-musical example of a point that cannot be missed can be described by the way the colorblind test works. The colorblind test is a picture made of red and green dots, with the red dots spelling out the number two, and the green dots providing the background. A person with normal vision will see the red number two clearly stand out against a green background, but a person who is colorblind will only see a field of gray. He taught me to apply the figurative colorblind test to every phrase I play.

Jerry was fond of telling me that while I was smart, my medulla oblongata (the reptilian part of my brain) was dumb. Since most of playing has to do with conditioned reflexes, it is necessary to *program* the reptilian part of the brain. In order to build trust with the reptilian brain, it's important to play entire movements or pieces many, many times. By doing so even the most difficult moves eventually become internalized. Before my Alice Tully Hall debut he had me play my entire recital program for him two or three times in a row. Eventually as soon as I played the first note of any piece, the whole piece seemed to set itself in my brain, and all the technical issues melded into the musical concept. Technique to Jerry was ultimately the physical choreography of a musical idea.

He also taught me how to internalize a phrase, and always insisted that I practice as much as possible in context. He encouraged me to hire pianists to make tapes of piano accompaniments, and he taught me the importance of playing along with recordings in order to physically feel the flow of a piece.

He taught me to use the very flow of the phrase itself to make a difficult maneuver, like a difficult shift, simply happen in the context of the trajectory (this works particularly well in the Schubert "Arpeggione" Sonata).

In spite of his brilliance and generosity as a teacher, Jerry Beal lived in a world of fantasy. He made things up all the time about his imagined career as a soloist. He often told me that he was going off to play a concerto with an orchestra like the Berlin Philharmonic under Herbert von Karajan, and he would even come back with recordings to prove it (whose recordings these were, I have absolutely no idea). This in no way marred my respect for his genius. In fact, it was because of this that he was able to lavish so much time and attention on me.

VII. SARAH AND FLORIA

During the New York run of the Royal Ballet Robert Gardner, the principal cellist of the New York City Opera, recommended me to be a finalist in an audition for the principal cello chair of the St. Louis Symphony. Bob was one of Leonard Rose's best students, but did not aspire to be the "next" Leonard Rose. He hated to practice, and rarely did. He didn't even want a decent cello. I went with him when he acquired his machine-made Juzak cello from Metropolitan Music, a wholesaler of cheap instruments. We tried a lot of instruments, and when he found the one that he thought was the best, he bought it for $125. I made him a gift of a $25 bow, an appropriate companion to this cello. If you have Stradivarius fingers you can make even a Juzak sound like a Strad, and Bob Gardner proved it to me. During his 46-year career as the principal cellist of the New York City Opera and the Aspen Festival Orchestra, he blended the voice of that Juzak with some of the greatest voices in the world, including those of Pavarotti, Domingo, Sutherland, and Sills.

His faith in me gave me the confidence to take this audition. As soon as I decided I was really going to concentrate on preparing for the audition, all kinds of physical problems seemed to evaporate.

I was doing double services every day at the Met, and had ten days to prepare for my audition. I practiced every night from midnight until I collapsed, and then I reported, bleary eyed, to the Met at ten o'clock for the next morning's rehearsal. I played a very good audition, and was sure that I would get the job. After the audition I got a call to audition for the principal chair of Sarah Caldwell's newly formed touring opera company called the American National Opera Company, so I decided to take it.

Sarah Caldwell (1924-2006) came to Boston from her native Arkansas as a violin and viola student at the New England Conservatory. She fell under the spell of opera in 1946 when she worked with Boris Goldovsky as a student at Tanglewood. She joined the faculty of the opera program at Tanglewood, spent eight years teaching in the opera program at Boston University, and founded her own Boston-based company in 1958. Her taste in opera went from the baroque to the avant-garde, and her staging was always spectacular. Her obituary described her as being a large woman of compelling personality who had fierce loyalties and fierce opposition, and one (unnamed) player is quoted as saying, "She makes you want to play better than you ever played in your life, and then she makes it impossible." Her administrative style was sketchy, she was reluctant to delegate authority, and she always spoke her mind. By the 1970s she was as identifiable a public musical figure as Arthur Fiedler, who conducted the Boston Pops. She appeared on the cover of Time Magazine in 1975, and was the first woman to conduct at the Metropolitan Opera.

I had only one day to prepare for my audition for Sarah Caldwell, and I was sure that I would have to play the *Tosca* solo because it was going to part of the tour. Unfortunately I didn't know the *Tosca* solo, and I didn't have the music for it. I called Bob Gardner, and asked him to sing it through for me, and I wrote it down on music paper. I practiced it for an hour, called him back, and played it for him over the phone to make sure I had it right.

The *Tosca* solo is very difficult because it goes very high and has large intervallic leaps. Because the sound quality of my instrument's A and the D strings matched perfectly when playing high on the fingerboard, and I was able to use the cross-string fingerings instead of jumping up and down the A string like people playing other cellos had to do.

I had my audition for Sarah Caldwell at the New York State Theater rehearsal room. After I played the *Tosca* solo she asked, "Could you play something else?" I played the *Tosca* solo a second time, and then a third, after which I said, "I know that you're doing *Tosca* on your tour, and this solo has a notorious reputation for sounding terrible. You just heard me play it perfectly three times. What else do you need to know?"

Since I was sure that I had the St. Louis job in my pocket, and feeling that there was nothing I couldn't do, I played half of the Bach Chaconne for her, and she offered the job on the spot. As it turned out I did not get the St. Louis job. This was actually very fortunate for me since my dyslexia would have surely done me in by the tenth or eleventh week of the season. Unlike opera and ballet companies, which do runs of 10-15 repeat performances, symphony orchestras change their programs every week. During the late 1960s orchestras would often play first (and sometimes only) performances of contemporary music. This would be a nightmare for somebody with reading difficulties.

The orchestra for the American National Opera Company was excellent, and had musicians from around the country. We held our rehearsals and first performances in Indianapolis, Indiana. The New York Philharmonic had a mandatory retirement age of 65 at the time, so Sarah Caldwell was able to engage flutist John Wummer and French horn player Rudolph Puletz, both retired principal players of the New York Philharmonic. Oboist Ray Still had been temporarily fired (for insubordination) from the principal oboe position in the Chicago Symphony and needed work until he was reinstated.

One day, during the time of Lady Bird Johnson's highway beautification program, we set up shop outdoors in a cornfield next to a junior high school to perform three scenes from *Falstaff*. While I was walking around checking things out with John Wummer, we noticed all sorts of goodies that were set out for the invited guests, including shrimp cocktails and a fair amount of alcohol. There was nothing for the musicians, and I asked John what he thought about that. His reply was that in Haydn's time, after the musicians played, they washed the pots and pans. He said that times have not changed.

The friendship I developed with Ray Still lasted throughout my career. During our bus rides he insisted on showing me all of his reed-making equipment, and would go on for hours about how he made his reeds, making it clear how important it was to have really good reeds. He invited me to play some Bach Cantata arias with him and a singer. I will always remember the sense of empowerment that I had playing with him. It was a lesson for life.

There were young players too, including Mary Lou Speaker, who became the principal second violinist of the Boston Symphony, and Sara Watkins, who became principal oboist of the National Symphony. Sarah Caldwell managed to get her tour classified as a credit course at the New England Conservatory, enabling men of draft age to stay out of the army (and Vietnam) for a while. Another contingent of players came from the Lyric Opera of Chicago, which was on strike during the 1967 season.

We had three operas in our repertoire: Puccini's *Tosca* (with Marie Callier and Peter Glossup, who had been engaged to sing at the Lyric), Verdi's *Falstaff*, and Berg's *Lulu*. Our *Lulu* was the first staged performance of the opera in the United States, and was seen by many noted musicians, including Leonard Bernstein.

I panicked when I saw the impossibly complicated music of *Lulu* at the first rehearsal. My assistant, Yuan Tung, encouraged me with comments like "You don't look too good," and "I'm worried about you."

When I returned to my "flea bag" hotel room, I knew that I would either master the many difficult *Lulu* solos or resign ignominiously. I knew that I could read anything if it was at a slow enough tempo, so I used the metronome and played every section at an extremely slow tempo raising the metronome up one notch at a time. By the time every section was up to tempo my rhythm, pitch, and sound were absolute, and I had many sections memorized. I followed this procedure for the next week, keeping myself slightly ahead of the progress of the orchestra. Many players in the orchestra complimented me, saying that I sounded like my teacher, Leonard Rose, and Yuan Tung stopped worrying about me.

Our conductor for *Tosca* was Jonel Perlea. Maestro Perlea was revered for his performances of *Tristan and Isolde* at the Met and for his many recordings. In 1957 he suffered a paralyzing stroke, which incapacitated his right arm. Being a man of steely determination he learned to conduct with his left hand and, according to Grove's Dictionary, "made a stirring impression in his performances of *Tosca* with the American National Opera Company in 1967."

These performances almost didn't happen. During one of the rehearsals for Tosca, Ray Still and Rudy Puletz made a scandalous scene antagonizing Perlea to such a degree that he tried to walk off the podium and resign. (Because of his stroke, he couldn't walk unassisted.) Later that day, I gathered three of my young colleagues, went to Perlea's hotel, and pleaded with him, saying that we young musicians would be deprived of a great musical experience we would never forget if he resigned. Maestro Perlea took the bait with alacrity, saying to his wife, "Yes! For the young people I will stay." Apparently he was looking for just such an honorable way of staying with the company.

I felt very fortunate to have played my first *Tosca* solos with Maestro Perlea. He conducted the cello quartet (one solo cello and three supporting lines) in two rather than in six, which greatly enhanced the wonderful harmonies. He congratulated me effusively after the first performance. Without thinking I said, "I did nothing but play in tune. The music all came from you." I could not have meant this more sincerely.

Maestro Perlea and I became good friends. He used to take me out to dinner after performances, and he took great delight in ordering me Brandy Alexander after Brandy Alexander until I was totally smashed. Many years later, when I played *Tosca* at the Lyric Opera with Julius Rudel, he asked me how Perlea had conducted it. Following my description of Perlea's way of conducting, he changed his interpretation and conducted the cello quartet in two. The next time Mr. Rudel came to the Lyric Opera he told me he had received many compliments on the national radio broadcast.

Marie Collier, the star soprano on the tour, came up to me one day and asked how it was that every cellist she had ever heard sounded pathetic on the Tosca solo, and I sounded so good. I explained to her that the unique quality that my cello had of being able to match the strings' timbre saved me from the usual search-and-destroy mission that other cellists experienced with this notorious solo. She said, "You must name this cello "Floria" in honor of Floria Tosca, the heroine of the opera." I did.

The American Ballet Theatre tour that March featured both *Swan Lake* and *Giselle*, so I played a solo every night for several weeks. Our concertmaster, who was also the contractor, had a fatal flaw. He was an adequate violinist, but he had a really bad sound, which he prominently displayed in *Swan Lake* night after night. He knew that this tour would lead to a big season at the Metropolitan Opera House, and he knew his playing would have been found unacceptable, so he came up with a plan to save himself.

He told the company that Tchaikovsky wrote these extensive violin solos for the court soloist Leopold Auer, who was the teacher of a whole generation of world famous violinists. He suggested that, in the spirit of the original intent, the company should hire great soloists of our generation to play these important solos.

Israel Baker was hired to play the solos when we performed in Los Angeles. Baker was an important violinist who recorded many chamber music works with Jascha Heifetz. At the end of the first Swan Lake performance, Mr. Baker approached me and suggested that I play for Gregor Piatigorsky and his students. Mr. Piatigorsky was a world-famous cellist; in fact, he was often mentioned in the triumvirate of Casals, Feuermann, and Piatigorsky.

There was a rivalry at that time between Piatigorsky and my teacher Leonard Rose, so I felt that by accepting this invitation I would be asking for trouble. I asked Mr. Baker why he thought I should do it, and he responded, "Let them hear what a real cellist sounds like." I was unable to resist such a compliment, so I said, "You arrange it and I will be there." Mr. Baker made arrangements for me to play for Piatigorsky at the Dorothy Chandler Pavilion a few days later

At the appointed time I showed up with my Boccherini Concerto piano part. I sat down to play the first movement, and in a very condescending voice Mr. Piatigorsky asked, "Why must you bore us with this piece, which is not even original Boccherini?" I replied that having studied with Luigi Silva for several years, I actually knew the original Boccherini Concertos, and thought this one was better than any of them. He said, "No, no, no, no. You must play something for my students so that they can learn from you. Play them the solo from *Swan Lake*, and then play them the solo from *Tosca*," which I did.

When I finished the *Tosca* solo he said, "You play this solo splendidly, but you do such funny things with your first finger." I said, "That's true. I bend it any way that keeps my finger on the note, and I sometimes even use my nail." "You use your nail?" he asked. "But this is infamous." "That may be true," I said, "but it enables me to play very fast." He asked me to show him, so I launched into the Popper "Spinning Song" at a very fast clip, playing the chromatic scales using down-bow staccato. When I finished you could cut the silence in the room with a knife. After a few pregnant seconds he said, "Young man, you have a charming smile," to which I replied, "Mr. Piatigorsky, you tell wonderful stories." Then he came over and gave me a big hug and said, "Young man, I want to wish you good luck," perhaps omitting the fact that I was probably going to need it. Then, he took up Floria and played very beautifully on her, commenting on her unusual construction and beautiful tone. As I reflect back on that incident I regret not showing this very great artist the respect that he truly deserved.

Chicago was the last stop on the tour, and one morning at 10:00 a.m. I got a call from Carol Fox, the general manager of the Lyric Opera of Chicago. She told me that she heard me play the solos in *Swan Lake* the previous night, and that she needed a principal cellist for her opera orchestra. She told me that she thought I was "it," and asked me to come play for her at noon. "That's fine," I replied, "but on two hours notice no Strauss or Wagner." She agreed.

I appeared at the stage of the now demolished Civic Theatre, and played for her and various assistant conductors for an hour. At the end of that time Ms. Fox said, "This is a decision that I simply cannot make by myself. My artistic director Pino Donati is flying in from Italy and will be here on Monday. Can you play for us then?" I agreed, providing she would pay for my ticket and a ticket for my cello to New York. She agreed.

My second audition lasted three hours. I started with the *Tosca* solo, of course. Then I played the Boccherini Concerto; the Prelude, Bourees, and Gigue from the C Major Bach Suite; solos from *Swan Lake*; the solo from the Brahms B-Flat Major Piano Concerto; two long variations from Strauss' *Don Quixote;* and some sight reading from the operatic repertoire: the Prelude from *La Traviata*, the opening of *La Boheme*, and the solo from *Don Carlo,* which are actually very easy (and I already knew how they went).

Pino Donati started to salivate over the sound of my cello, exclaiming over and over again in Italian, "What a beautiful cello." I called out to Carol Fox, "Please tell your friend that I come with the cello." The audition ended with Strauss' *Don Juan*, which I knew by memory. I ceremoniously pushed the stand to one side, and launched into the opening, which I botched up. Carol Fox said, "That will do." I replied, "That will not do," and I played it once again, this time acing the passage. I continued to play for a page and a half, at which point she yelled out, "Uncle! How much money will it take for you to live in the style to which you would like to become accustomed?" I said, "Make me an offer." She said, "Three hundred and twenty-five dollars." I said, "Three fifty," and she said, "Done."

Although I didn't mention it before, Sarah Caldwell had a very unsavory reputation because she was most odoriferous, and because her checks constantly bounced. Carol Fox was extremely interested in any denigrating comments I might have had about my experiences with her, which were many. It was on this common ground that Carol Fox and I became instant friends.

Carol Fox managed to get Maria Callas to make her American debut in the first season (1954) of the Lyric Opera by traveling to Italy and offering Callas $1,750.00 per performance. Rudolph Bing, General Director of the Metropolitan Opera, had a policy that no singer would ever make more than $1,500.00 per performance. Carol Fox's offer was irresistible to Callas. Eventually, Bing came to Chicago to ask Callas to sing with the Metropolitan Opera at her price. Danny Newman, the director of public relations at the Lyric Opera said that it was the greatest surrender since Lee surrendered to Grant at Appomattox.

Danny Newman was born in 1919 in Chicago, and served in World War II where he fought in the Battle of the Bulge. He owned movie houses, was active in the Yiddish theater, promoted the drive-in movie craze, produced radio programs, and created the subscription-based business model that is in use all over the world. He began as the Lyric Opera's publicity director in 1954 and continued there until shortly before his death in 2007.

* * *

The new Metropolitan Opera House at Lincoln Center was less than two years old when the American Ballet Theatre took up residence there for its July 1968 season. The season featured *Swan Lake* and *Giselle* very prominently, giving me fantastic solo opportunities, and Aaron Rosand was hired to do the big violin solos from *Swan Lake*. Rosand liked my playing and became my advocate, recommending me for everything he could think of. Because of my dyslexia, I found ways to get out of accepting the recording dates, but when he recommended me to be the cellist of the Reston Trio with his long-time friend Elliot Magaziner as the violinist, I accepted happily.

The orchestra had many distinguished players, including both concertmasters of the Metropolitan Opera, and one of its principal oboists was William Arrowsmith. My stand partner was John Goberman, who was also the assistant principal cellist at the New York City Opera. At some point John decided that being a professional cellist was not satisfying, so he convinced the powers that be to let him start a project of televising major performances from Lincoln Center. This was the beginning of the PBS series "Live from Lincoln Center," which featured the New York Philharmonic, the Metropolitan Opera, the New York City Opera, and the American Ballet Theatre.

Our principal conductor was Kenneth Schermerhorn, who I had worked with during my very first American Ballet Theatre tour. Over the years that I worked with him I found Kenny to be a truly great conductor. He always reminded me that the test of a real artist is to be able to make a second- or third-rate work sound great. Playing solos with Kenny conducting was always a joy. Before he left the American Ballet Theatre to become the music director of the Milwaukee Symphony, Kenny made a special arrangement of *Les Sylphides* (music by Chopin) where he gave the most beautiful melodies to the solo cello.

VIII. MY FIRST SEASON AT THE LYRIC OPERA

There were three weeks between the last performance of the 1968 American Ballet Theatre season and the first rehearsal of the Lyric Opera. The first opera of the season was *Salome*, and I knew that much of my future depended on how well I played the cello part, so I devoted every waking moment either to practicing the part or listening to the opera. I actually "notched" every passage on the metronome until my fingers could play everything without any participation from my brain.

Leonard Rose once told me that no one can absolutely guarantee success in any given performance, but there are many things that one can do to put the odds in one's favor. Since I believe that there is no excuse for a bad solo, constant practicing was my way of putting the odds in my favor.

At my first Lyric Opera rehearsal I met Lois Bickel Colburn, a cellist in her late 60s or early 70s. She had been my predecessor Shirley Tabachnick's teacher, and had four former students in the cello section of the Chicago Symphony. She gave the Chicago premiere of the Kodály Unaccompanied Cello Sonata, and was a member of the first string quartet to perform all the Bartók quartets in the American Midwest.

She must have viewed me with a certain disdain and suspicion when I arrogantly announced that I would play the *Tosca* solo better than anybody had in the history of Chicago. I did eventually win her over when *Tosca* came up early in the season, but she told me not to break my arm patting myself on the back. This was only one of her many tangy phrases. She said about one of our conductors, "What he knows about music you can put in your eye *and see better*." About the cello section, minus the two of us, she offered the comment, "They add up to a big round zero *without the rim*." Years later when Bruno Bartoletti conducted the Ritual Fire Dance from Manuel de Falla's *El Amour Brujo*, her response was "Jesus wept." Whenever it looked like I might get myself into trouble, she advised, "When the devil says good morning, tip your hat."

She had emphysema, caused by a lifetime of smoking, and had shoulder problems. Since the best defense is a good offense, she had something bad to say about everybody, and she did it in grand style. She would call the younger players "junior geniuses," and some of the older colleagues who talked too much were "IN-sufferable!" When Joe Saunders, my stand partner, asked her to listen to him play and criticize it, she said there was a lot to criticize. I'm sure that once was enough for Joe. On the other hand, she really liked me, and encouraged me to play as loud as I could and let them know what I could do, but also encouraged me to go back and study with Leonard Rose because he was "Mister Big." There wasn't anything exceptionally dramatic about our friendship, but we shared our time together every day in a spirit of love and appreciation, and I treasure the memory of my time with her.

Lois was good friends with the great American luthier Carl Becker and his son Carl Jr., so she took me to their shop so they could meet me and have a look at my cello. Carl Jr. told me that this cello could never project more than five feet away, and I would do very well to commission a new cello from him. I played the cello solo in Verdi's *Masked Ball* about a month after this visit with the Beckers, and Carl Becker, Jr. greeted me at the stage door to tell me how beautiful my cello solo was. I asked him where he was sitting, and he said in the top balcony. I mentioned the fact that this was a good long city block from the pit, and reminded him that he had told me the cello wouldn't project more than five feet, to which he replied, "Life is full of surprises."

Pinchas Steinberg, our concertmaster, was an unforgettable character. Pinky was only twenty-three years old when I arrived. After studying with Heifetz and Gingold, he held the position of principal second violin of the Cincinnati Symphony before he came to the Lyric. He was born in Israel, and could speak at least five languages fluently, which came in very handy over the years since so few of our conductors (many of whom were French, German, or Italian) spoke English well enough to communicate everything they wanted to.

Pinky's greatest aspiration was to conduct, and he proved heroic during a performance of *Don Giovanni*. Our conductor, Ferdinand Leitner, was overcome by the noxious fumes emanating from the stage when Don Giovanni descended to hell. Pinky immediately leaped to the podium and conducted the final scene of the opera perfectly from memory. In 1970 when Christoph von Dohnányi failed to appear for the first rehearsal of *Der Rosenkavelier*, Pinky was able to conduct the entire first rehearsal without any problem. It was perhaps this experience that hastened his departure from the Lyric Opera after only three years. He left us to study conducting with Herbert von Karajan, and made his debut with the RIAS Symphony in 1974. His career as a conductor is impressive, and he regularly appears in the most prestigious opera houses and concert halls in the world.

Christoph von Dohnányi, the grandson (and student) of the Hungarian composer Erno Dohnányi, made his American debut with the Lyric Opera in 1969 with the *Flying Dutchman.* He returned for consecutive seasons conducting *Salome, Rosenkavalier, Masked Ball,* and *Cosi fan tutti.*

Bruno Bartoletti was the Lyric Opera's music director and principal conductor. He was born in Florence in 1926, and studied flute and piano at the Florence Conservatory. He made his conducting debut with a performance of *Rigoletto* at the Teatro Comunale in Florence, and over the years introduced many important contemporary works to the Italian stage, like Ginastera's *Don Rodrigo,* Kreneck's *Jonny Spielt Auf,* and Shostakovich's *The Nose.* He first came to the Lyric Opera in 1956, and became the principal conductor in 1964.

His conducting technique was nonexistent, but his ability to make an orchestra sound great was undeniable. I spent more than 38 years with him at the Lyric Opera of Chicago, and this never changed. I found it fascinating that he was able to conduct amazing performances of Alban Berg's *Wozzeck* and Dmitri Shostakovich's *Lady Macbeth* without any kind of technique. His rehearsal method was to constantly drill the motivic material, asking for the highest degree of rhythmic precision and emotional commitment, and he would often start at an extremely slow tempo and work the material up to speed. This kind of rehearsing was possible in the late 1960s and early 1970s, because the Lyric Opera contract gave him excessive amounts of rehearsal time every week. Nothing of the sort could ever be done in the 21st century.

Antonino Votto had been Toscanini's assistant at the first performance of *Turandot*, and he conducted it by memory when he came to the Lyric. Once, when I played a wrong but plausible note in a solo, he commented, "Well, that's another opinion." He was a wonderful man and totally non-dogmatic. Argeo Quadri was another great conductor, and his 1969 and 1970 performances of *Madama Butterfly* were amazingly beautiful. Only Daniele Gatti came close to equaling his interpretation.

In 1968 Placido Domingo made his Lyric Opera debut in Puccini's *Manon Lescaut.* His Manon was Renata Tebaldi, the most famous soprano of the golden age of opera, rivaled only by Maria Callas.

Domingo went on to become one of the greatest tenors of the later 20th century, rivaled only by Luciano Pavarotti. The dress rehearsal was stunning, but the performance never took place. Renata Tebaldi contracted the Asian flu and was too sick to sing, so she canceled the entire run. This was the only time in the history of the Lyric Opera that a performance was canceled. Carol Fox substituted *Don Pasquale* until a new soprano could be found. I found it absolutely astonishing that anyone could be too sick to perform, until I got the Asian flu. That was about as sick as I've ever been.

June didn't come with me to Chicago, and I found myself very depressed and lonely when I wasn't working. I called Bob Gardner every Sunday, and he gave me good advice about how to handle the job and the depressing aspects of loneliness. Fortunately June got a job in the opera orchestra for the next season, and we were together during the opera seasons from then on.

Carol Fox, the person who hired me as the principal cellist of the Lyric Opera, and hired June as a member of the violin section, invited me to lunch at the Tower Club when I was in Chicago with the American Ballet Theatre in 1969. I mentioned that I had a friend who was a conductor. She replied, "Everybody has a friend who's a conductor." I said, "However, not everybody's friend who's a conductor is George Szell's assistant at the Cleveland Orchestra and knows 30 operas by memory." In dismissing my comment out of hand, she missed the opportunity to engage James Levine at the beginning of his career.

After a few years as principal cellist of the Lyric Opera, I felt richly entitled to a raise. When I explained to Miss Fox that I was definitely worth more money than I was making, her reply was, "Danny, I don't think I can find a better principal cellist than you, *but* I have a dollar amount in my head for how much I will pay my principal cellist, and if you go one penny over that, I will do less well." I responded by saying, "There are two things that I know. I know that you know how much you *can* pay me, and I know that you are fair." She gave me a $100-per-week raise, which was a lot in 1971.

IX. PERSONAL TRANSFORMATION

In June of 1969, thanks to the recommendation of Aaron Rosand, I was engaged by the Northern Virginia Music Center as artist-in-residence and a member of the Reston Trio. My responsibilities involved coaching the cello section of the student orchestra, playing the Dvořák Concerto with the orchestra, and playing six chamber music concerts. I found this assignment daunting because at that point I had played exactly one serious chamber music concert in my life, and the idea of playing a concerto on the same series as Aaron Rosand made me very nervous.

My colleagues in the Reston Trio were pianist David Poliakine and violinist Elliot Magaziner. During World War II David Poliakine had been a prisoner in a Japanese camp as a result of being at the wrong place at the wrong time while on tour, but he met his wife, a woman with a Dutch-Indonesian background, there. He was well known as an accompanist for both Michael Rabin and Aaron Rosand.

Elliot Magaziner was a staff violinist at CBS, where he shared a stand with Aaron Rosand. Elliot had sound advice about performing. He told me that you should "expect to bleed if you get out on the stage," which I interpreted as expecting to play your best under pressure is futile. He told me that the reason so few people actually get out there is that they are afraid to bleed. It was with this kamikaze-like attitude that I was able to put myself, scared half to death, in front of an orchestra and play the Dvořák Concerto for the first time.

At the first rehearsal I expressed my doubts to James Christian Pfohl, the conductor of the orchestra, about the ability of these young people to play the difficult orchestral score competently. James responded by telling me, "If you don't tell them they can't, they can." Well, they could, and they did, splendidly. I learned a lesson about how to be a teacher.

The summer was a positive and successful time for me, but the nervousness that I felt at the beginning continued. Elliot's enthusiasm for our piano trio possessed him to book Carnegie Recital Hall for two concerts the following March and May, which caused me some anxiety. I was 29 years old, and I had not yet played a New York recital that had been reviewed in the *New York Times,* a professional rite of passage. I had read many career-destroying reviews of concerts by people I knew were good players, and I worried endlessly that I might shortly join their ranks.

The year between September 1969 and September 1970 was a year of personal transformation. My emotional stability took a downward spiral between the time that I went back to the Lyric for the fall season and the first concert of the Reston Trio in Carnegie Recital Hall in March. My new assistant, Joseph Saunders, who had been a member of the Chicago Symphony under Fritz Reiner for twelve years, had a lot to say about my various orchestral inadequacies. It annoyed him that I could convincingly fake a difficult passage and get a smile from a conductor like Christoph von Dohnányi, while he, having played all of the notes, and having gotten behind because he dragged, received a look of severe rebuke.

Joe once invited me to his home for dinner and played me a recording of a mediocre performance he gave of the Beethoven A Major Sonata. He resented my obvious lack of enthusiasm, and from that point on, every time I played a solo he would tell me how various principal cellists messed up the very one I was playing. I got so mad one day that I told him whatever these paragons of cellistic virtue may have screwed up in his presence, he could forget about ever hearing me mess up anything.

I put on a brave show, but the specter of Carnegie Recital Hall, the *New York Times*, and Joe's constant negativity eroded my confidence, and I started to have severe anxiety attacks.

There were many positive things about this season. The first opera that we did was Mussorgsky's *Khovanshchina*, with Nicolai Ghiaurov, one of the greatest voices I would ever hear at the Lyric Opera, in the lead role. Listening to Ghiaurov helped me to improve my cello sound in the lower register. I believed, up to that point, that the cello simply sounded asthmatic when it was played melodically on the G and C strings. When I imitated Ghiaurov's voice during the passages in the opera when the cello section played in unison with him, my sound in the lower register improved dramatically. Puccini's *Madama Butterfly* was the next opera that impressed me during that season. Those incredible melodies ran through my head constantly as I walked to and from the opera house. It was difficult to believe that such music could actually exist. Two great tenors I heard for the first time that season were the magnificent Richard Tucker and Alfredo Kraus. Piero Cappuccilli over time became my very favorite baritone.

X. BOLTS OF LEITNERS

When Ferdinand Leitner came to the Lyric Opera to conduct *Don Giovanni* we became friends almost instantly. Like my teacher Leonard Shure, Leitner had been a piano student of Artur Schnabel, and like Shure he found the only way to be a real artist was to ask the music at all times what it demands, and find a way to satisfy those demands technically. He was born in Berlin in 1912, and studied composition at the Berlin Hochschule für Musik with Franz Schreker and conducting with Brahms' student Julius Prüwer. He became Fritz Busch's assistant at Glyndebourne in 1935, and began his conducting career in Berlin in 1943 at the Theater am Nollendorfplatz. In 1947 he became the director of the Stuttgart Opera, and helped make that city one of Europe's leading centers for opera. He left his position there in 1969 to become director of the Zürich Opera, and came to conduct us often.

Some conductors think of themselves as performers, but Leitner considered his primary responsibility to be a teacher. Over the years, and through persistent effort, he single-handedly turned the Lyric Opera Orchestra into a great-sounding Wagnerian ensemble. I feel fortunate to have played almost all of the Wagner operas with him, as well as several operas by Strauss and Mozart.

In spite of Leitner's annoying habit of staring at anyone who made a mistake (we used to call these stares "bolts of Leitners"), he was one of the most loved conductors in the history of our company. We always gave him our best. While many conductors could instantaneously fix up anything that went wrong, nothing ever went wrong in a Leitner performance. He had a quiet demeanor and never seemed to have to fan the flames to get things going.

During the many intermissions I would spend with him, we would ponder whether Schubert might have evolved any further had he lived longer, since the level of greatness in his music composed in the last two years of his life made him practically the equal of Beethoven. I would play the cello solos from Strauss' *Don Quixote* for him, and he would sit at the piano and play the rest of the score from memory, telling me what Strauss said about this, that, or the other thing. My favorite quote from Strauss by way of Leitner was, "Music from Mozart on is a large diminuendo, and I am the dot at the end of it." I suppose that after composing *Elektra*, Strauss decided that the next step would be in the direction of Schoenberg, and that was definitely not for him. Another thing that Leitner did for me, something unique in my forty-four-year experience with the Lyric Opera, was to get me an important European manager for a European tour I was planning. The tour never came to be, but I am still pleased to have been the third cellist on a roster with Rostropovich and Fournier.

John Pritchard made his Lyric Opera conducting debut with *The Barber of Seville*. Pritchard was very famous for his interpretation of Mozart's operas, and I was fortunate to work on *The Marriage of Figaro*, *Cosi fan tutti*, and *Don Giovanni* with him. He was the only conductor who was willing to sit with me for as long as it took to work out the important solos in *Don Giovanni* and *The Masked Ball*. He was actually willing to deal with cello-related considerations, and I was willing to acknowledge the needs of the vocal line. He told me about positive reactions to our work on these solos (actually duets between cello and singer) from Daniel Barenboim and Renata Scotto.

After that opera season I went back to New York and rehearsed with Elliot and David in preparation for those upcoming trio concerts in Carnegie Hall and went on an American Ballet Theatre tour that ended only a week before the first Carnegie Hall concert. As the tour progressed, my anxiety increased. The only time I felt "normal" was while I was playing the cello solo in *Swan Lake*, because there it felt normal to be nervous.

When the tour got to Chicago, I received a phone call from Carol Fox asking me to come meet her for lunch. I arrived at her office in the Opera House, and she told me that my stand partner, Joe Saunders, had called her and told her that I had suffered a nervous breakdown and couldn't play anymore. She told me that he asked her, "How do you know when we're both playing, who's really doing the playing?" Carol assured me if she didn't know the difference between his playing and my playing, she would resign as general manager of the Lyric Opera immediately. She had been to the Ballet, and she thought I sounded every bit as good as I ever had. She then and asked me what the problem was.

I explained to her that I was apprehensive about my upcoming New York concerts with the Reston Trio, and that I was concerned about what the nasty critics from the *New York Times* would say about me in print. I thought, perhaps, it would be better if I canceled the concerts and waited for a more propitious time to stick my neck out. She then gave me some excellent advice. She said, "Danny, listen to me. I deal with artists all the time, and I can tell you that canceling is an easy habit to get into, and a hard one to break. You go and play those concerts, and know that whatever they say about you in the *New York Times*, good, bad, or indifferent, I will welcome you back with open arms."

When I returned to New York, armed with Carol Fox's excellent advice, I threw myself into practicing and rehearsing, and played the first concert. The Trio received a tepid, but somewhat positive review. The second concert of the Reston Trio featured a trio written for us by Nuncio Mondello, who was a jazz saxophone player. The cello part to this trio was the hardest thing I ever had to play, and I worked on it incessantly in between the two concerts. The second concert got an even more tepid review with a couple of nasty cracks from Donal Henahan, the nastiest and most feared critic of the *New York Times*. The experience of surviving these two concerts lifted my depression. It actually sent me off in the opposite direction. I felt, after playing the frightfully difficult Mondello, that there was nothing that I couldn't play, so I attacked Schubert's "Arpeggione" Sonata with gusto. I decided I was ready to make my New York solo debut.

I performed the "Arpeggione" Sonata for the first time in Reston that summer, and also played the Haydn D Major Concerto with the orchestra. Elliot played a very impressive performance of the Paganini D Major Concerto with the famous Sauret cadenza, and David played Beethoven's Third Piano Concerto. We performed the trio repertoire we had played in New York, and added a few pieces, like the Tchaikovsky Trio. Working with Elliot Magaziner bridged the gap for me between being an amateur and being a professional chamber music player, and I will always be grateful to him for his uncompromising and hard-nosed approach to showing up and doing your job.

XI. CASH FOR A GUADAGNINI

My friend Gil Solomon told me that Sam Eisenstein, a New York luthier, had some pre-World War I bridges, and he suggested I get one for Floria. I went to Sam's studio on 57th Street, played my cello for him, and talked him into giving her one of those bridges. Sam was impressed with my playing, but he thought that I needed a cello that would make the floor rattle when I played on the C string, like a great Montagnana or Gofriller. I told him that while I would love to have one of those fantastic instruments, I did not have the fantastic amount of money required to buy one. Sam decided to make it his mission to find me something that I could afford that would sound like a great Montagnana or Gofriller. Over the years, he would call me up with various things that came in, but none of them really suited me or sounded better than Floria. In the meantime, Sam kept her sounding spectacular.

Lois Colburn, my former Lyric Opera colleague, desperately wanted me to have her Carlo Antonio Testore cello, so in early 1970 I flew to her home in Houston, picked up the cello, and gave her a check for $7,500, which was all the money I had in the world. I was anxious to have it appraised by an expert, so I brought it to the famous luthier Jacques Francais. I expected him to ooh and ah over my acquisition, but no such luck. Francais told me unequivocally that this was a French cello made by two different makers. He said that he was saving my life by telling me this, and saving me from this fraudulent purchase. Francais and Sam Eisentein had studios in the same building, so I went down to Sam's studio, and told him what happened. He was not surprised, and told me in his usual blunt fashion that Francais was full of shit, and if I brought it to Wurlitzer, another New York dealer, I could expect to hear the same thing. Sam was sure the cello was a Testore, but, he said, "Sound is your department, and this cello will never sound. There's oil in the wood. Get rid of it."

A week before the beginning of the 1970 Chicago Lyric Opera season Sam Eisenstein called to tell me about a cello he wanted me to try. I went down to his studio, played three notes on the cello, and then said two words: "How much?" He replied, "$6,000 in cash." *That* I could afford.

Sam and I went to the bank. I had never dreamed of taking $6,000 in cash out of a bank. I felt like I was guarding Sam's life with the $6,000 in his pocket as we wended our way back to his shop. I tried the cello with one of his bows, which I really liked, so he threw that one in for $250, plus a case. I made my career with this equipment, and to this day I continue to play this cello. After 41 years of abuse, the bow finally cracked at the tip. Unfortunately the damage was irreparable.

My new cello was made by Gaetano Guadagnini (Gaetano was the son of J. B. Guadagnini, and the teacher of Joseph Rocca and Pressenda). From that day forward I played the Guadagnini for all my recitals, all my solos in the ballet and the opera, and I used it to make all my recordings. It has a C string that makes the floor rattle, and even when I was playing my absolute best, I never felt that I had come to the end of its potential. I have never felt the need to upgrade, even when I was offered first crack at Leonard Rose's Nicolò Amati. With this cello I felt confident about planning my New York debut, and I decided the newly-built Alice Tully Hall at Lincoln Center was the best place to perform.

Alice Tully (1902-1993) could be considered the polar opposite of Rebekah Harkness in the spectrum of patronesses of the arts. Her mother was an heiress to the Corning Glass Works, and her father was a state senator. Her motivation to become a musician came at 14 when she heard the pianist Joesef Hoffman play a recital, and after several years of studying voice in New York, she spent seven years studying in Paris. She made her debut in 1927, and appeared in a production of *Cavalleria rusticana* in New York in 1933. She continued to sing until 1950, when she felt her voice was losing its flexibility.

After inheriting the family fortune in 1958, she turned her efforts to philanthropy. She served on the boards of the Metropolitan Opera, the New York Philharmonic, and the Juilliard School of Music, and was a trustee to many of New York's museums. She gave most of her financial support, many millions of dollars, to these and to other institutions anonymously. Her cousin Arthur Houghton, Jr. was one of the founders of Lincoln Center. Shortly after Miss Tully (she never married) inherited her mother's Corning fortune, Houghton asked her if she would be interested in financing a chamber music hall for the Juilliard School of Music's new building in Lincoln Center. She agreed, but did not want her name to be associated with it, just in case the hall ended up with less than ideal acoustics. John D. Rockefeller III persuaded her to reconsider after hiring Heinrich Keilholz to design the acoustics.

Since she spent a good deal of her time sitting in uncomfortable concert halls in America and in Europe, Miss Tully wanted this hall to be comfortable. She selected the colors for the walls and the fabric for the seats. She also made sure that there was adequate leg room for the people sitting in its 1,086 seats. The hall opened on Miss Tully's 67th birthday, September 11, 1969.

My mother's friend Cecile Martindale was the assistant to Omus Hirschbein, and Omus Hirschbein ran one of the most successful concert series in New York at Hunter College. She told me that you couldn't play a New York recital without having a manager, so she got Hirschbein to recommend me to a New York manager named Sarah Tornay. I was filled with joy, and was sure that I had absolutely arrived. In this particular case, however, dogma triumphed over common sense.

Common sense told me that giving a New York recital involved a list of things that simply had to be done: booking a hall, getting a flyer printed, getting an audience, and getting a review in the *New York Times*. I couldn't understand why having a manager would be necessary to complete these steps. Cecile assured me that I wouldn't want to be dealing with details right before I had to play. I decided on Saturday, May 15th as a date, and assumed that Sarah Tornay would take care of everything.

When I returned from Chicago after the 1970 opera season, I called Alice Tully Hall to make sure that my date was set. Nobody there had ever heard of me, and the booking agent told me that May 15 was already booked. I asked her about May 22nd, which was open. I asked her what I would have to do to book it, and told her that I could supply reviews and letters from conductors, to which she replied, "Just bring a check."

During my final year at Juilliard I heard Paul Olefsky play two stunning recitals in Carnegie Recital Hall within the space of a week, and studied with him during the next summer. Paul had been the principal cellist of the Philadelphia Orchestra for four years, and the principal cellist of the Detroit Symphony for six. He also was a winner of the Naumberg Competition, and had a very successful career as a soloist. I played for him often over the next several years, and his critical advice changed the course of my life and established my career.

I always thought that you needed to win a contest to be considered credible enought to appear on an important New York stage. Paul Olefsky assured me back in 1966, when I considered resigning from my position at the American Ballet Theatre in order to enter several competitions, that my professional accomplishments made me as credible as any competition winner. "There are lots of competition winners without jobs, and the job you have can be a stepping stone to a better job." He mentioned that Leonard Rose hadn't won any competitions when he made his debut, and that Emanuel Feuermann hadn't either.

Armed with my checkbook, I went down to Lincoln Center, gave the woman a check for $750, and went to the front of Alice Tully Hall to check out flyers for upcoming concerts. I noticed that Sheldon Soffer's management had the best flyers. It was obvious to me that if I reacted so positively to Sheldon Soffer's flyers, which were even better than the ones from Columbia Artists, a flyer of that quality should make me look as good as any artist on those top-of-the-line rosters.

I went to the pay phone in front of Alice Tully Hall and put in a call to my good friend Henson Markham. Henson was the rental department manager for the music publisher Boosey and Hawkes, and knew everything and everyone connected to the music business. I asked Henson if he could find me the name of the graphic designer that Soffer used, and in five minutes I had Walter Harper's telephone number, so I called and went right away to his 12th Street apartment.

Walter Harper was an aspiring tenor. We had a lot to talk about since by that time I had played with many great tenors at the lyric, including Richard Tucker (who I believe is unrivaled as a dramatic tenor), Alfredo Kraus, and Placido Domingo. Walter asked me for a picture, so I put in a call to my mother and asked her to bring a sketch she had of me at the cello (someone made it during a concert) that was to become my lifelong logo. Together we came up with a design that I have used for all my flyers and all my recordings. In a period of about eight hours, I had a hall and a design for a flyer: two of the major items required.

The next item of business was to get an audience. I asked Danny Newman, the person who built the subscription audiences for the Lyric Opera of Chicago and many other performing organizations, for advice. In his inimitable style, he told me, "Take your destiny into your own hands. Write to everybody you have ever known: people from kindergarten, people from first grade, people from high school, people whose names you can barely remember, and invite them to this important event in your young life." I wrote 250 letters, using both sides of the page, inviting all these people to come as my guests, and I encouraged them to bring as many friends as they wanted. Who could resist going to a recital at the newly-opened, and very important, Alice Tully Hall played by someone they knew?

I had the first full house, to that date, for a debut recital in the history of Alice Tully Hall. I got a good review in the *New York Times*, and an even better one two weeks later, when I played another recital (to another full house) in Carnegie Recital Hall, where I played the Brahms E Minor Sonata and the Clarinet Trio with pianist Elizabeth Wright and clarinetist Alfred Loeb. Alfred was the principal clarinetist of the American Ballet Theatre orchestra, and he split the expenses connected with putting on this second concert. I wanted to do it as a kind of insurance: if I failed at Alice Tully Hall I would have another chance to get up on a New York stage right away.

I was plagued with right arm problems when I gave my next solo recital at Alice Tully Hall the next year. Shortly after arriving at the hall, I noticed that I was producing a tremor in the middle part of my bow that made me self-conscious and nervous. I considered canceling the concert. I looked in the mirror in the room back stage and thought, "This is my concert, and I can cancel it if I want, but I'm pretty sure I can get through the Boccherini A Major Sonata, so I'll go out on stage and play that." The Boccherini went fine, and the Beethoven A Major Sonata that followed it also went fine.

The next piece was the Bach Fifth Suite, and I had a memory slip in the fugue. I calmly started the fugue again, but I had another memory slip in the same spot. I started the fugue once again, and once again I had the same memory slip.

I considered my options, looked out at the audience, and announced, "I'm going to give it one more try." The people in the audience laughed, and I even started to laugh. I started the fugue one more time, and, sure enough, I made the same memory slip, but this time I knew what it was and how to proceed. I finished the fugue and finished the piece without incident. Peter G. Davis of the *New York Times* gave the concert a wonderful review, mentioning only that perhaps, due to an unsettling memory lapse, the fugue seemed a little slack.

Like every other debutante, I found myself worrying about what the critic was going to say about my playing. In order to save my sanity I decided that it was my job to play the concert, and his job to write the review. It was *not* my job to write the review while playing the concert.

I had only two weeks after my first Alice Tully Recital to rehearse the Brahms E Minor Sonata and the Clarinet Trio. There's a passage in the slow movement of the Clarinet Trio that involves a large leap that I just could not make reliably. I decided that if I were to miss the shift, everyone would know, but if I played the passage an octave lower, there was a good chance that nobody would notice. I took the second option, and was rewarded by being dubbed a "first-rate cellist" by Donal Henahan, the "terror" of the *New York Times*. I wonder what he would have said if I took the first option and missed the shift.

XII. AMERICAN CHAMBER CONCERTS

I came into the 1968 American Ballet Theatre season playing way over my head, and attracting a lot of positive feedback from my colleagues after my appointment as the principal cellist of the Chicago Lyric Opera. At one point in the season, June's stand partner Joyce Robbins (the sister of Channing Robbins) took me aside and suggested to me that if I wanted to have a happy marriage I should make sure that June also had a career.

She was absolutely right. June and I formed a piano trio, and we made a commitment to play exclusively with each other. By so doing, we gained many professional advantages and personal pleasures. Since we were married and we played in the same opera and ballet orchestras, we had the same schedules, so we could always find time to rehearse. We could bring a unified conception and a polished execution to rehearsals with our pianist.

June had a love and a talent for management. She was responsible for setting up American Chamber Concerts and for getting almost all of our dates. June and I were also able to finance important concerts in New York, so we could move effortlessly from one project to the next without being compromised or restricted by outside parties or the need for money.

After my two big concerts in the Spring of 1971, I decided to stay in New York and play the summer American Ballet Theatre season rather than return to Reston. When the school at Reston folded the next year, I made a proposition to Samuel Aschelman and Rosalyn Capen, the owners of the Coolfont Recreation and Conference Center that hosted student concerts at the end of the summer. I suggested that they should continue their series with professional musicians (like June and me). They liked the idea.

We needed to find a pianist, and Peter Basquin accepted our invitation. We didn't know it when we asked him, but Peter had just won the Montreal International Competition. We would not have dared to ask him if we had known. After the ABT season, the three of us drove down to Berkley Springs, West Virginia, and played four concerts. This began our 33-year association with Coolfont. (The Coolfont Center closed down in 2004). Our series at Coolfont was extremely important to us because it was through our performances there that we were able to perfect all of the programs that we would take on tour and play in New York.

Sol Hurok was one of the most famous managers of the time (and perhaps of all time). He began his career managing Isadora Duncan and Feodor Chaliapin, and through his Russian connections and his chicanery, he got the exclusive rights to bring the Bolshoi Ballet, David Oistrakh, Mstislav Rostropovich, Leonid Kogan, Emil Giles, and many other musicians and dancers from the Soviet Union to New York during the Cold War. For many years June and I played in the orchestra for all of the Hurok attractions that came into New York.

In 1973 Hurok lost the contract to bring the stars of the Bolshoi to the Metropolitan Opera House, and the contract went to the Niederlander Management. Niederlander hired a trumpet player named Mitchell Jellen to contract the orchestra. June and I had played with Mitch for years, and we thought he was our friend. For that reason, I was extremely surprised when he told me that he had many friends, and consequently was not going to hire us for the New York season.

Since we were ungainfully employed for the spring of 1973, June and I decided to work on our solo and chamber music repertoire, and play as many concerts as we could. Every Sunday we would play a concert somwhere, even if it was only at a suburban library for five or ten people. Gordon Steel was our pianist, and our program never varied. I played the Francouer E Major Sonata, June played the Debussy G Minor Violin Sonata, then we played the Brahms B Major Trio, and after an intermission, we played the Kodály Duo. We would also speak to the audience about the music we were playing. We found this to be a very effective way of getting re-engaged. When we played at Heritage Village, a senior citizen's home in Connecticut, I told the audience, "Brahms was a meticulous composer. It is a well-known fact that he destroyed 75% of his compositional output. We are going to play you one of his failures. You might ask, 'Why would we play a failure when there were so many successes?' The answer is, at the end of his life Brahms took this early B Major Trio and completely revised it, combining the inspiration of his youth with the genius of his maturity." We were re-engaged eight years running, and at good fees.

I decided to audition for Affiliate Artists, an institution that paired musicians with communities. The pay was $1000 a week for 10 weeks, and being part of this venture was considered a major boost to one's credibility. I was determined to get one of these fellowships, and practiced assiduously for six weeks.

The first round of auditions was held in Carnegie Recital Hall, and I played absolutely brilliantly. No doubt about it. The next person who came to audition after me actually fell off the fingerboard during the first run in the Adagio of the Boccherini A Major Sonata. This cellist had been my stand partner during a run of the Bolshoi Ballet at the Metropolitan Opera House. His mediocrity was no secret to me. I knew that I had aced the audition, and I was sure that I would get the fellowship. It was hard for me to believe that he got the fellowship and I didn't. It was a bitter pill to swallow.

June put this defeat into perspective. She said, "What would have happened if you had gotten Affiliate Artists? You would have 10 weeks of concerts and $10,000, and good-bye. If we had a management, we could probably generate concerts year after year, and you would be beholden to no one."

The American Ballet Theatre Choreographer Lar Lubovitch created a ballet called *Scherzo for Massah Jack* to the some of the music in Charles Ives' Piano Trio. I performed it at least 20 times with ABT, so I was very familiar with the cello part. June, always the adventurous one in our family, decided to learn the whole Trio and start a project of playing Ives' music. 1974 happened to be the 100th anniversary of Ives' birth, so we prepared a program of Ives' music that included the Second Violin Sonata, the Piano Trio, and a few piano pieces, and the National Gallery of Art invited us to perform on a concert celebrating the Ives Centennial, for which we got a good review in the *Washington Post*. We performed the same program a week later in Chicago at the Museum of Contemporary Art.

We decided, as an experiment, to book the New York Cultural Center for a series of three concerts, and booked Carnegie Recital Hall for a two-concert series the next year. Our success with all of this encouraged us to incorporate ourselves as "American Chamber Concerts." We observed that although there were many artists, there were only a few managements, so we created a three-person board (the legal minimum), consisting of me, June, and my best friend Joseph Jacobson. Joe was a college book salesman who traveled all over the country. He worked hard to get us dates wherever he was selling books. We also hired (for $10 an hour) an executive director to talk with presenters on the phone and type letters and contracts.

I learned a great deal from my experiences with American Chamber Concerts. I learned that if you have to ask somebody to do something, that person's interest in you is absolutely tangential. A musician is a commodity that can be replaced very easily by another musician. It does not matter to a manager who (or whom) they represent, as long as they get their 20% and a retainer. I also learned that if 100 people try out for one job, there would be 99 losers. Rather than waste the time and energy involved with diving into a competitive arena, it's much better to create your own opportunities using Robert Ringer's "leapfrog theory," that states, "No one has an obligation, moral, legal, or otherwise, to 'work his way through the ranks.' Every human being possesses an inalienable right to make a unilateral decision to redirect his career and begin operating on a higher level at any time he believes he is prepared to do so."

Does it really matter whether you win a contest to play a recital, or if you put one on yourself? For many years, I watched the winners of many competitions play to small audiences on Tuesday or Wednesday afternoon concerts at Town Hall. I did not have the bragging rights of having won these competitions, but I certainly had bigger audiences, and many times I had better reviews.

Contrary to conventional wisdom, I found that the fewer associates you have (as long as they are capable and loyal), the better off you are. The reason for this is that a career is based on long-term gains, and you have to last a long time in order to have the results. I can't say that I had the kind of success that most young people dream about, but I did play a lot of concerts. I also got many good reviews, and I recorded the repertoire at the level that I wanted to. I was beholden to no one, because my interests and those of my colleagues were totally aligned.

A career consists of the concerts that you play, the recordings that you make, the jobs that you hold, and perhaps the contests that you win. It is not necessary for all of these things to happen simultaneously. Each part can be achieved separately and put together later in a package.

I once ran into my neighbor Frank Solomon, the very famous manager of the Marlboro Festival and the People's Symphony Concerts at Washington Irving High School in New York, while he was walking his dog. He asked me about a particular conductor he had heard at the Lyric Opera. I told him, "If you take him, you will make a lot of money." He replied, "That's not the only thing I'm interested in." I replied, "In that case, I think he's a three dollar bill." At that point, in a moment of extraordinary candor, Frank said to me, "I want you to know, you're doing the right thing by managing yourself, because no manager will ever work as hard for you as you will work for yourself."

XIII. CHANNING ROBBINS AND LEONARD ROSE

After the American Chamber Trio made its Carnegie Recital Hall debut on April 5, 1975, June and I both decided to take lessons. It ended up being the best possible thing for both of us because two of the greatest string players of all time lived in New York and were available to teach us.

David Nadien is one of the finest violinists to ever play the instrument. He won the Leventritt Competition in 1946, and Leonard Bernstein appointed him as the concertmaster of the New York Philharmonic without an audition. He stayed there from 1966 until 1970, when he left because commercial work in New York was more lucrative. We first met him when he played the solo part of the Chausson *Poème* with the American Ballet Theatre orchestra, and found that he had a couple of quirks that separated him from mere mortal violin players. He never warmed up, and he could make the cheapest violin sound like a Stradivarius.

He was willing to teach professionals like June on Sunday afternoons, as long as they were willing to pay his hourly rate for recording sessions. He totally revised June's technique, very much for the better. Her sound and articulation improved significantly, right from the start. He would assign her various concertos from the repertoire, and spend the lesson putting in bowings and fingerings, explaining as he went why he had chosen those fingerings and bowings, and demonstrating how he used them. In the five years that she studied with him, June said that he taught her how to think on the violin.

Leonard Rose was one of the greatest cellists of all time, and the greatest cello teacher of his day. Nearly every major American orchestra can boast having had a Rose student as its principal cellist at one time or another. When I first studied with Mr. Rose in 1957, he was curiously concerned with proper grooming. In late 1950s teenage boys still groomed their hair with the goal of having a "plastered-down" look. Much to my chagrin, Mr. Rose was very concerned about my pompadour and the glue I used to get it properly placed. He also insisted that I wore socks that wouldn't fall down, particularly in the middle of a performance. He often asked me about how I was doing in high school, and one day when I came in with a black eye, he asked me what the other guy looked like.

He cared a great deal about how I played, and was unwilling to allow me to have anything in my blossoming repertoire that he hadn't heard. When I told him, for example, that I had already played Romberg's Second Concerto, he still insisted on hearing me play it for him before he would let it go.

Mr. Rose was insecure about the unpredictable income he made from giving concerts, so William Schuman, president of the Juilliard School of Music, offered him a teaching contract in order to relieve his financial worries. In 1957, when I was studying with Mr. Rose at Juilliard, he was contracted to give 15 students 30 lessons a year at a rate of around $25 a lesson. Since Mr. Rose was a man of unbending integrity, he insisted on giving all these lessons in spite of the fact that he was often exhausted. There were times after he returned from a tour that we would get three lessons in three consecutive days.

After the third of three such lessons, he came up to me in the hall and asked me if I had anything else to play for him. One of Mr. Rose's students canceled his lesson, and he didn't want to let the hour go. I was amenable, so he dug into my music case and found the cello part to the Schubert B-flat Trio. I exclaimed to him that it was only a the cello part of a piece of chamber music, so he picked out the most difficult passage and told me to play it for him. Unfortunately for me (in retrospect), I played it perfectly, so, instead of getting a valuable lesson on how to play one of the great masterworks from one of the greatest cellists, we spent the rest of the hour talking.

Mr. Rose mentioned that he wouldn't want any son of his to be a professional cellist because it was too difficult a profession. He told me I should be a doctor and make money. When I asked him whether he thought I didn't have sufficient talent to do the job, he replied honestly, "If you think that you're going to have a career like mine, forget it. There were many people of extraordinary talent that were my contemporaries that never made it. I was the only one who did." I asked Mr. Rose how far he thought I could go, and he prophesied that I would probably be the principal cellist of a good orchestra and would play a lot of chamber music. That was fine as far as I was concerned (and it even came true). In spite of his prediction, I always knew that I would go as far as I could, and take advantage of the opportunities that presented themselves to me, period.

I vividly remember the enormous amount of energy Mr. Rose put into trying to get me to extract every ounce of beauty that I could from the instrument. In my junior year of high school I was the principal cellist of the New York All-City High School Orchestra. I had a very big cello solo to play in the Overture to Lalo's *Le roi d'Ys*, which I brought to a lesson. When Mr. Rose played the solo for me, he went into an almost ecstatic state, and in one particular place at the end he played an upward whole-tone shift, first finger to first finger, from a G natural to an A natural. The combination of the timing, the delicacy of the sound, and the vibrato were truly transcendent. I can still picture him playing those two notes, and can still feel his intense desire to impregnate me with the indellible impression. The sound and the gesture made an enormous emotional impact on me, and I was able to replicate it in the performance we gave in Carnegie Hall. It was an effect I have used from that point forward, and I always carry in my heart.

I am still amazed at the generosity of spirit that motivated him to give so much of himself to a 16-year-old kid. He was at the pinnacle of his early solo career, and made remarkable recordings of the Saint-Saëns Concerto and Bloch's *Schelomo* with Dmitri Mitropoulis and the New York Philharmonic, the Brahms Double and Beethoven Triple Concertos with Bruno Walter. His recording of the Schubert "Arpeggione" Sonata, the Boccherini A Major Sonata, and sonatas by Sammartini, Grieg, and Franck proved that as a cellist he had no peers. The beauty of his sound, his emotional warmth, and the intelligence in the phrasing, were, and still are, unmatched.

In 1959 Mr. Rose reduced the number of lessons he was able to give in half, and he hired Channing Robbins and Luigi Silva to divide up the other 15. Mr. Rose held a high regard for Mr. Silva, but he had no idea that his regard was *not* reciprocated. I first chose to work with Channing Robbins, which ultimately was a very, very good choice.

Channing Robbins was 36 years old in 1958, and I was his first student at Juilliard. He had a positive influence on me in every way. He thought I was abundantly talented, and he told me so. Channing showed me clever exercises to do to fix my bow arm, something that Mr. Rose was not able to do. He was a font of information, and could talk at length about the great pedagogy of Feuermann, Felix Salmond, and D.C. Dounis that educated and inspired me for my entire lifetime.

I was so happy with my work with him that I continued to take lessons after the spring semester at Juilliard ended and before I went to

Blue Hill to study with Silva for the summer. When I went back to study with him 17 years later, he fixed my bow arm again, however, the price for a lesson went up from $6 a lesson to $25.

I wanted Mr. Rose to consider me the top of the pack, but it was clear that, for whatever reason, he thought other students were more talented than I was. I happened to meet Luigi Silva at Joseph Settin's violin shop while I was in a state of consternation about Mr. Rose's preferences. Mr. Silva played some Paganini Caprices for me, and I was duly impresed by his technical display. I asked him whether he thought he could teach me to do that, to which he replied, "I don't know." I spoke with Mr. Rose about working with Mr. Silva, but rather than dividing lessons between the two teachers, I decided to to go the whole hog and just study with Mr. Silva. Mr. Rose believed that Silva was an authority on the left hand, and that I could learn a lot from him, so I made the switch.

I believe that Luigi Silva had been looking for a student with my degree of talent for a long time for the sole purpose of proving that he was a better teacher than Mr. Rose. He lavished time and effort on me, teaching me how to achieve pyrotechnical ability by working through books and books of very difficult etudes. During lessons he denigrated Rose as somebody who "had to start six months in advance on one of the passages in the Dvořák Concerto to play it in tune." Of course, the fact that Rose played the Dvořák Concerto better than anybody else ever had never occurred to me, but what I did know was that Mr. Silva was going to teach me how to play better than my competition.

I became an advocate for Mr. Silva, and I tried to convince many Rose students that they would be much better off studying with him. Mr. Silva sent me into my Juilliard jury (to be judged by Ivan Galamian, Joseph Fuchs, Mr. Rose, and himself) with his transcription of the Vitali Chaconne, the very difficult Locatelli Sonata, the Brahms E Minor Sonata, the Barber Concerto (a piece Rose played the previous year with the New York Philharmonic and claimed was the hardest piece ever written), and a Gruetzmacher Concertstucke.

The Barber Concerto has a very difficult passage in parallel thirds which I could play better than Leonard Rose because I spent a whole year practicing exercises in thirds with Luigi Silva (Leonard Rose even cut out a couple of thirds when he played it). When this passage came up in my jury, Mr. Silva stopped me to say that, "Mr. Rose is thinking that maybe you played some of those thirds out of tune. Would you please play them again and show him that this isn't the case?" After I played the passage perfectly a second time, Mr. Rose, who was boiling mad, exclaimed "Danny, I'm telling you this in front of your teacher: don't you ever dare snub me again."

The snub happened the day before my jury when I met Leonard Rose in the hall. He asked me whether the Greutzmacher piece I was playing was any good. My sententious reply concerned the fact that since Greutzmacher was the person who wrote the Boccherini Concerto, and since that was a good piece, this must be too. Then he wished me luck playing the Barber Concerto. My reply to his kindness was to say, "If I can play it, I don't need good luck. And if I can't, I don't deserve good luck." "In that case," he said, "Bad luck!"

What I ultimately got from Luigi Silva was a great deal of tension in my playing that took me ten years to repair. I could say that studying with Luigi Silva was a total disaster in my life, except there were two good things I got out of it. Mr. Rose was right about Silva's *conception* of left hand technique. It was quite good, and it helped me to survive during my initial years in the profession. The second good thing was that I met my wife June on a blind date that Mr. Silva's son set up. June clearly had a much greater and enduring influence for good in my life than Silva had for bad.

Eventually I realized the gravity of my mistake, and decided that it was crucial for me to get back into Rose's good graces, and I came up with a plan. Whenever anyone in any of my touring cello sections would compliment me on my playing, I would always mention that I owed everything to studying with Leonard Rose. We always hired a few extra cellists in every city we visited so word spread far and wide. I hoped that word would eventually reach Mr. Rose, and as I became more and more successful his impression of me as a student might be more positive.

Before my debut recital at Alice Tully Hall I naturally sent Mr. Rose an invitation and flyer, and I also wrote him a note to thank him for all that he had taught me. Elizabeth Wright, the pianist I played with, did a great deal of accompanying in Rose's studio at Juilliard, including accompanying the 16-year-old Yo-Yo Ma. After receiving my invitation, Mr. Rose asked Liz whether I really could play the "Arpeggione Sonata," and she told him I played it about as well as she had ever heard it. When I walked out on the stage of Alice Tully Hall, who should be staring straight up at me from the first row? It was none other than Yo-Yo Ma, flanked by his two parents. Mr. Rose wrote me a letter to voice his approval, and told me, "Incidentally, you're making excellent programs. Real cellists' programs. Markedly devoid of attention-getting, worthless modern crap."

In 1975 Mr. Rose agreed to work with me again, and he accepted my long-overdue apology for my 17-year-old snub by saying, "People change, and it's a good thing that they do. You've changed and I've changed, and I'm truly grateful that you came back to me, because I never could have come back to you." According to Dean Acheson, Harry

S. Truman's Secretary of State, "Nobody ever comes out second best in his own memoirs." In this case, I clearly came out second best to Leonard Rose.

When I played the Haydn D Major Concerto at my first lesson, I was so nervous that I could hardly keep the bow on the string. Mr. Rose looked at me in astonishment and said, "I don't understand how it's possible for you to be the principal cellist of two major orchestras, and play recitals at Alice Tully Hall, if you get so nervous." I replied, "I can deal with the nerves of playing at Alice Tully Hall, and certainly the solo responsibilities at the Lyric Opera and the American Ballet Theatre. However, I thought you would be insulted if I didn't get at least this nervous playing for you." He laughed, and said, "Nerves only hit you where you're weak, and you're weak in your elbow." He then gave me a demonstration about how to use the bow, something that I have elaborated on in my book, *Fundamentals of Cello Technique and Musical Interpretation,* published by the International Music Company.

He wouldn't accept any money. He told me to take the money I would have paid him to Max Frirsz and have him make a new bridge and soundpost. He confessed to me that he felt like an adulterer going to Frirsz because Erwin Hertel had helped him get his Amati cello. Then he said, "My ears hurt when I played the cello with that new bridge and soundpost."

Mr. Rose told me that Frirsz would charge me twice as much as anybody else, but that I would not really be paying for a bridge and a soundpost. I would be paying for how much better my cello will sound. He was certainly right about that. In compensation for future lessons, he was willing to take a gratuitous bottle of scotch.

Since I could only work with Leonard Rose when one of his Juilliard students would cancel, he suggested that I should work on a regular basis with Channing Robbins, his long-time assistant. Channing Robbins knew more about how to play the cello than anybody I ever met, and he could answer any question I asked him. Since he charged $25 a lesson I would take four lessons a week, when I had the time. Leonard Rose pointed out the weakness in my bow arm, but Channing transformed it into a bow arm that really worked, almost without my knowledge of the process.

I became obsessed with the idea that I could only be a legitimate cellist if Leonard Rose said so. I was interested in José Silva's method of projecting a picture of something I wanted to happen, so for 20 minutes a day, I would sit with my eyes closed and picture Leonard Rose saying all kinds of nice things about me.

The American Ballet Theatre presented the first televised complete *Swan Lake* on June 30, 1976, which was one of the first *Live from Lincoln Center* presentations. I managed to play the solo in the second act extremely well, and a few days later, a colleague informed me that Leonard Rose had seen the broadcast, and had many complimentary things to say about the anonymous cellist in the second act solo. Whether or not this approbation transpired because of my meditations is an open question, but it did radically change my relationship with Leonard Rose. Perhaps if he had known that I was the cellist in that performance, he would have thought about it differently, but after hearing it he showed me a degree of respect that had not been there before. One of the greatest moments of my life happened when Leonard Rose asked me for an autographed picture.

At the end of the 1976 American Ballet Theatre summer season, June and I received a call from the WQXR host Robert Sherman. He told us that he had discovered Rebecca Clarke, a wonderful British composer, and was very keen on popularizing her music. Sherman asked if we would be willing to take part in a radio show he was putting together to celebrate her 90th birthday. Toby Appel and Emmanuel Ax were hired to play her Viola Sonata, and Sherman wanted us to play her piano trio, which had never been performed in New York.

Rebecca Clarke's international success as a composer began in 1919, when her Viola Sonata won second place in the American patron Elizabeth Sprague-Coolidge's Berkshire Prize competition. It continued when her Piano Trio was awarded the second prize in same competition in 1921. Clarke, who was also a very fine violist, divided her time between London and New York between the wars, and moved to New York in the 1930s, where she remained for the rest of her life. She stopped performing after her marriage to James Friskin in 1944, and wrote her last known piece in 1954. People stopped paying attention to Rebecca Clarke and her music until Robert Sherman re-introduced it to his radio audience.

As a result of Sherman's interest, both the Viola Sonata and the Piano Trio became extremely popular, and have even become staples of the repertoire. After the radio premiere, through which we got to meet the composer, we gave the first performance of the trio on a New York stage in Carnegie Recital Hall in 1978. We still have the manuscript parts in our possession.

1976 was also the first time I played with the pianist Eric Larsen. Peter Basquin, the pianist of the American Chamber Trio, was unable to play two run-throughs in preparation for the Carnegie Recital Hall concert we scheduled for the season. He recommended Eric as his replacement for the run-throughs, and we became instant friends. I was engaged to make a videotape of a recital for a cable station in Los Angeles, and I enjoyed our musical rapport so much that I asked Eric to play with me for the television program. Over the next 35 years I performed the cello and piano repertoire almost exclusively with him, and in 1987 Eric became the pianist of the American Chamber Trio.

During the 1976-1977 American Ballet Theatre season there was a rumor about that Loren Glickman was going to be the new contractor for the orchestra. Those of us who were long-time players were not exactly sure that Glickman was going to hire us, so we decided to organize an ad-hoc orchestra committee. Jim Stubbs, the principal trumpet player, Porter Poindexter, principal trombonist, and I went to the offices of Local 802 of the American Federation of Musicians and asked Max Arons, the president of the union, whether he would recognize us if we organized the orchestra. He responded enthusiastically, saying, "I've been waiting for this for years!"

We held a meeting on the last day of the season. We organized the orchestra, and got a strike vote on the issue of instantaneous tenure for everyone there. This included 45 players, who played at the New York City Center. Jim Stubbs and I thought that as long as we were going into the Metropolitan Opera House with an orchestra of 56 players, we should have a tenured orchestra of 56 players. One of the proudest moments of my life came at a meeting with management at which I was able to say that we were either going to have an orchestra of 56 tenured players at the Metropolitan Opera House, or the American Ballet Theatre was not going to go into the Metropolitan Opera House. This is a case in point that proves my theory that if they can screw you, they will screw you, unless you can legally prevent them from doing it. Because of this action, my wife June and I had secure and gainful employment for the next 21 years.

Jim Stubbs became the contractor for the American Ballet Theatre orchestra in 1980, and he gave me *carte blanche* to appoint people to the cello section whenever there was an opening. This happened quite often because the players I engaged were so good that they were always leaving for better jobs elsewhere.

The Lyric Opera had its difficulties. Carol Fox, the person who hired me, nearly ran the company into the ground. The company's three million dollar endowment shriveled down to only $6,000, and a 1978 production of Penderecki's *Paradise Lost* combined with 25th-anniversary celebration in 1979 sent the company into a $1.2 million deficit. After pressure from the Lyric Opera's board of directors, Carol Fox resigned in 1981.

Ardis Krainik (1927-1997) became the new general director of the company. She was a mezzo-soprano who began her career at the Lyric as a secretary to Carol Fox. She sang some minor roles, and then became an artistic administrator for the company in 1960. Without any formal training in finance, she was able to turn the company around financially.

She restructured the company's operations, reduced the number of orchestra rehearsals, and borrowed stage sets. By 1993 the company was back in the black, and the company was even able to buy and renovate the Civic Opera House. She also added contemporary music to the repertoire, and commissioned new works by European and American composers.

XIV. DR. ALBERT ELLIS

One of the unfortunate side effects of my second Alice Tully Hall concert was a severe and debilitating case of tendonitis in my right arm. This condition plagued me for the next several years, and had it not been for the psychological help given to me by Albert Ellis, my career could have come to an end at age 31.

There was no tenure at the American Ballet Theatre, and I did not want anyone to know that I was experiencing numbness in both my bow arm and my left hand. I had many solos to play and the uncertainty of whether or not, or how, they were going to go was extremely troubling. At the suggestion of Laura Curtis, a great patron of the arts who hosted many play-through recitals for me in her home, I contacted Dr. Albert Ellis.

Dr. Ellis (1913-2007) was the chief psychologist for the state of New Jersey in 1950, but because he published many books on human sexuality, served as the American editor for the *International Journal of Sexology*, and was a known advocate for sexual freedom (he was the first prominent psychologist to advocate gay liberation), he was unable to find a teaching position in New York. He thereby had to make his whole income from private practice. He charged $25 for a half-hour session (far less than other New York psychotherapists of the time), and streamlined his approach so that those 30 minutes would really count for his clients.

He saw so many clients that he could make note of characteristics he saw in the basically "neurotic" but otherwise non-mentally-ill people who came to him for help. He observed that most unhappy people are handicapped by irrational and rigid thinking, and that most people are fully aware of it, but they hold onto their beliefs even if those beliefs continue to make them unhappy. He combined this observation with the teachings of Stoic philosophers (like Marcus Aurelius), and taught his clients that all neurotic emotions come from a person's view of a particular situation and not from the situation itself. Dr. Ellis also delighted in being as iconoclastic as possible, and he used curse words as liberally as he could think them up.

Dr. Ellis explained, during our first meeting, that my number one problem was interpreting the events of my life as awful. Awful, he explained, hasn't any limit. Bad, you can deal with.

The first item in my litany of woe was that my arm was driving me crazy. He responded by telling me, "No! You're driving you crazy. Your arm just hurts. Now, what's the problem?" I told him that I had an extensive solo to play that night at the ballet, and I wasn't sure if my arm was going to crap out on me. He asked how long the solo lasted, to which I responded that it was about two minutes long. He asked me how much I had played so far today, and I told him that I had played about two hours, and he said, "It's hardly likely that you couldn't play for two minutes if you have already played for two hours, and even if you couldn't, don't you have an assistant who you could alert to cover for you? And even if you were to play badly, you imagine your colleagues will think that you've crashed and burned, when in reality they'll just think that you're having a bad day."

That evening I played that solo and many other solos perfectly well, and I was surprised that my level of playing was actually better than it had been, mostly because of the increased amount of focus I brought to bear at the moment of truth.

Another session concerned my fears about playing the very difficult cello parts in Wagner's *Die Walkure* and in Berg's *Wozzeck*. I was afraid that with the large amount of rehearsal time we had the conductors might spend a lot of time taking things apart. I was worried that if they found me substandard they would do everything in their power to humiliate me. I also told him about my dyslexia, and how hard it was for me to read and figure out difficult music quickly.

He responded, "My dear, you are the principal cellist of this opera company. It's your job to play those notes, and if you don't, it's their job to make you feel bad about it. Furthermore, is there any reason why between now and next week you couldn't put in two hours a day figuring out this music? You might even find that after you start, a certain automaticity will set in, and the work will go a lot faster."

This turned out to be exactly the case. I did the work, and made an excellent impression when I returned to the Lyric Opera. His advice effectively changed the way I thought about myself. Before seeing Dr. Ellis I felt like a victim, and I was afraid that conductors were dead-set on humiliating me and criticizing me. After considering Dr. Ellis's explanation that conductors were just doing their job, the same way I was just doing my job, I felt much less afraid to go into a rehearsal. I knew that I had a choice to make: do my job, or accept the fact that if I didn't, the conductor would have to do his job.

Among other things, Dr. Ellis insisted that I record all these sessions so, as he put it, "I don't have to keep saying the same thing over and over again." He gave me a "present" to take to Chicago. It goes like this:

1. Something is bothering me. I wonder what it is.
2. I know what it is, but is it true?
3. If it is true, what's the evidence to support it? If it isn't true, what stake do I have in believing something which is untrue?

My friends all thought I was crazy when I told them that after being the principal cellist at the opera for five years I was still nervous about *how* to do the job. They thought that it was impossible not to be able to do a job that I had been doing successfully for five years. Dr. Ellis's response was different. He told me that there were all kinds of things that he couldn't do, and would never be able to do well. He gave the example of statistics, which is a necessary part of the study of psychology. He told me that he just had to deal with it, and that he did the best he could without that particular expertise. He told me that you can compensate for your liabilities to a degree, but you only need to compensate for them to the degree that gets you over the top of what you want to do, and that the rest of the time, you can play your strengths to the hilt.

Once I came in complaining that I had played something really badly. He asked me why I didn't enjoy playing badly, and went on to say that if you have an instrument in your hands and music to play, and things aren't going well, you can always listen to what other people are doing. He told me that I can do the best that I can do, and that I can enjoy the process of transforming something bad (i.e. my playing that day) into something good.

In response to my complaint about having to ingratiate myself to people I didn't respect in order to safeguard myself (there was no tenure at the ballet), he asked me why I should feel bad about it. He told me that I didn't make the rules, and suggested that if I was playing by the rules, the rules are the game. He told me that if I was playing the game to win, following them doesn't say anything about me except that I can keep my job and make money.

Sometimes his advice was extremely practical. When I told him I had been engaged to do a summer festival between the ballet season and the next opera seasons, he told me to get a substitute for the summer festival because I needed to harbor my strength, time, and energy for the opera season, which is much more important.

These sessions helped to sustain me for the next three years when I had to play at a high level while being physically handicapped. Dr. Ellis taught me that I could deal with reality, but not with fantasies of disaster. He liked to say that it's not what happens to you, but your opinion of what happens to you that will determine how you feel and how you act.

I even went with June to Dr. Ellis so that he could help us work out some "issues" we had when we first began to work together in the American Chamber Trio. June felt that I was being too rough on her, and I felt that it was my job to bring her up to snuff. Dr. Ellis told June that if she were to go out on a stage and be criticized by the people hearing her play, she should do as much as possible to sound good. He convinced me that I should make her sound as good as possible, but I should do it in a way that addressed musical and technical issues without getting personal about it. We spent two hours with Dr. Ellis, and it was the best $100.00 investment I ever made in my life.

Channing Robbins had an interesting psychological approach to teaching. He gave me technical tools, and I used them faithfully to work through the difficult repertoire I played. Once, when I called Channing at 7:00 a.m. before leaving for a concert in South Carolina, he helped me a great deal by telling me, "I know that you're going to do it your way, but you'll do it better because you learned to do it my way." When faced with playing the Brahms Double Concerto and the Beethoven Triple Concerto, I asked him why my bow arm was falling apart. He told me to go home and play the slow movement of the "Arpeggione" Sonata in the lower half of the bow without any motion in the fingers, and come back to see him at 6:00. When I came back, the problem was solved. He said, "Celebrate. Now that you solved this problem, if it ever comes up again, you'll know how to handle it."

Perhaps the most valuable thing that Channing taught me concerned time and energy management while on tour. He taught me the mindset of practicing while I was playing on stage, which was very helpful because it saved a lot of energy and the relative detachment of practicing rather than performing put me in a calmer state of mind than I would have ordinarily been in. He told me that the audience wouldn't know the difference. He also told me that it is useful to pay attention when things are going well so that you can replicate the feeling when things are going badly.

I played my program for my third Alice Tully Hall recital for Channing, and asked him whether I should begin the first piece on the program softly or loudly, he told me to play it loudly and "show them who's boss right away." When I played the "Arpeggione" Sonata for him, he told me that it sounded well played-in. With that statement he made one of the most difficult pieces in the cello repertoire feel like a comfortable old shoe.

I was never sure if Channing Robbins actually liked me or just put up with me, since I had a tendency to contradict him. After he died his sister sent me an autographed picture of Jascha Heifetz, dedicated to Channing Robbins. Both Channing and his sister were part of the children's orchestra in the movie *They Shall Have Music* that featured Heifetz playing the last movement of the Mendelssohn Concerto. He gave every child in the orchestra an autographed picture as a gift, and the fact that Channing Robbins had given this very personal gift to me was a vindication that our work together had pleased him.

XV. DYSLEXIA AND ITS DISCONTENTS

Henry Winkler ("The Fonz" from *Happy Days*) was denigrated as being an underachiever as a child, and is one of many people who has had difficulties with dyslexia throughout his life. He mentioned in an interview that you don't get over dyslexia: you just learn to deal with it.

I wasn't able to read words until I was nine years old, and was only able to do so with the insistent help of my father. I have never been offically diagnosed with dyslexia, and have therefore never received proper therapy for it. Translating difficulties with dyslexia into musical terms seems to be rather rare, and because I kept it a secret for my entire professional life, I have no method for comparison with other musicians. I imagine that most people like me compensate by using their ears rather than their eyes to translate what they see on the page into sound.

A lot of orchestral cello parts are relatively easy, and sounding great while playing sustained notes makes a tremendous impression. It is also rather easy to hear harmony from the bottom up, and it is rare that the bottom of a chord gets drowned out by the notes above it, unless you want it to be drowned out. Whenever the cello section has 16th notes or 32nd notes (I think of them as "herds of zebras") they are almost always doubled by the violins or drowned out by the brass. The main responsiblities of being principal cellist have to do with playing beautiful solos and interacting rhythmically with incision and bite. I happened to be good at those particular skills, and consequently if anything was said against me, conductors would have attributed it to professional jealousy rather than my shortcomings.

One of the things that I learned in my first opera season playing *Salome* is that "something is always better than nothing." There is a quintuplet passage in that opera that I could somehow have faked, but instead of faking it, I converted it into patterns that fit my hand, and I organized the patterns into groups of four 16th notes per beat. When I played it in context I simply made sure that the first note of every beat was the one that Strauss had put in the original part. I ended up sounding better than anybody else, and I sounded better in every important way: I was louder, more incisive, and better in tune. I could drown out the whole cello section because I was absolutely sure of what I was doing, when my colleagues were not.

I simply did what was necessary to be able to deliver the goods at the moment of truth any way I could. I listened to recordings endlessly, and I practiced difficult passages very slowly. I would repeat the passages at incrementally faster tempos, going notch by notch on the metronome until they were at the required speed. I would make recordings of myself playing exposed cello passages, and I would repeat each passage six times. I would then play many times with the resulting tape, which would allow me to play exposed cello passages in operas and ballets with a level of reliability and panache that conductors always appreciated.

When I had tricky syncopations in contemporary music, or when I had passages to play at speeds beyond which I could actually hear, like those in Alban Berg's *Lulu* and Michael Tippet's *Midsummer's Marriage*, I used the half-speed dial on my now-antiquated tape recorder to record accurate versions of myself playing the passages. I would then play along with the resulting tape at full speed. This enabled me to train myself to play by ear rather than by eye.

When there was the possibility of being covered up by the violins, or if I could be kept in line by other instruments playing the same music, I would fake shamelessly and save my energy for the parts that were truly exposed.

In spite of my severe reading difficulties, I survived (and actually thrived) as a principal cellist for half a century. My father was very fond of saying, "Some people are cheered on as they race through every test, get straight A's in whatever they try to do, and find themselves at a dead end. Others are marooned and shipwrecked for years, but eventually get to where they need to go." I definitely fit into the latter category.

XVI. DIE MEISTERSCHLEPPERS

Eric Larsen was working as a staff pianist at the North Carolina School for the Arts when I first began playing with him, so our touring together involved working around his academic schedule and my opera and ballet schedules. It always involved schlepping, and we considered ourselves "Meister-schleppers." Traveling with just two or three people and a cello has its inconveniences, but traveling with a ballet company and a cello has inconveniences that nobody could imagine.

Natalia Makarova joined the company in 1970. She and Mikhail Baryshnikov, who both defected from Russia, were very important. The two of them brought the American Ballet Theatre to the top of the ballet world. When we would tour, Natalia Makarova insisted that she should be the first person on the airplane, something contrary to the FAA's determination that my cello should go on the airplane first. The way we solved the problem was for me to put my cello on the plane, strap her in, and then remove myself from the plane and take my place among the lowly musicians. Makarova could then lead the dancers onto the plane in all her glory.

In January and February of 1981, Eric and I went on a three-week-long tour that began by car in Asheville, North Carolina. We had a rough trek through the mountains in an ice storm between Winston-Salem, where Eric's school was located, and the University of North Carolina in Asheville. We arrived at the auditorium 30 minutes before the concert and found that it was freezing cold. Nobody had turned on the heat. I had no idea how I would play the "Rococo Variations" or even the Beethoven Sonata we programmed. I reminded myself that faith is not the ability to believe in spite of the evidence, but the willingness to act, regardless of the consequences. Thanks to the spotlights on the stage, the hall got warm enough for me to play comfortably.

Eric's car broke down after our second concert at Queens College in Charlotte, and after his fan belt was replaced we made it to Duke University. Because I was a bit nervous, I had a nice shot of vodka before the performance. Giorgio Ciompi, the first violinist of the faculty quartet, came by to wish me good luck, but he wasn't interested in drinking vodka with me. Perhaps because I was so well lubricated, I played way over my head (a lesson that was not lost on me in the future). I had a problem with my bow at our North Carolina School of the Arts concert, but was able to have it repaired by the concert we played on Valentine's Day at SUNY-Purchase. My old friend Walter Hagan was in the audience, and after the concert we talked about old times. I was very sad to learn that he died shortly after that concert.

Aside from having a motel room right above a heavily chlorinated swimming pool when a flight was canceled due to bad weather, the rest of the tour went without incident. We decided to call our adventure, "Nothing but the best."

Between 1982 and 1986 there were airlines that issued tickets offering unlimited mileage for a period of three weeks for just $500. This was great for the trio because for a $2,000 investment (three people and a cello, which had to have a seat), we could play for very low fees and still make money. One problem with this arrangement was that for domestic flights on Delta, the "hub" had to be Atlanta, Georgia. Even if we flew from Los Angeles to San Francisco, we had to go by way of Atlanta, so we spent a lot of time in the Atlanta airport. Sometimes we would find an empty boarding area to sit down and practice the music we were playing that night.

One company called People Express didn't have bulkheads, so my Guadagnini had to go in baggage (they told me that People Express transports people and not cellos). After some negotiation, they allowed me to put the cello in the baggage compartment myself, and they let me get off early to take it out. In between, they served me three vodkas. Fortunately, nothing bad happened to the cello. I can't say as much for my nervous system. Perhaps the only drawback of having unlimited mileage tickets was that if we didn't make our connections we would have to pay full price for regular tickets for three people and a cello.

Touring always involves dealing with unexpected difficulties as well as surprises. We began one tour to the American Midwest by leaving our music in a cab, and we had to spend most of the night before our first concert writing fingerings and bowings into a second set of parts we traveled with, just in case. Our first concert was in Illinois, and though our luggage ended up going to Detroit, we were able to play because we brought our music stands, dress clothes, and instruments on the plane with us as carry-on items.

We once had back-to-back concerts at two schools in Louisiana: a fancy school for white girls, and one with all African American students. We were told that the concert at the second school, a program of Schubert and Ravel, would be drowned out by boom boxes, but we were pleased to find our advisor proven wrong. The audience was extremely attentive.

We used our unlimited mileage for international tours as well as domestic ones. We hired a manager for our tour of South America, and we agreed to play as many concerts as he could book for us in a two-week period. He got us unlimited mileage tickets on Varig Airlines, and had us playing in a different city practically every day.

Concerts in South America began at 9:00 p.m., and the South Americans liked to have parties after their concerts. We were, of course, required to attend these events, even if we needed to be at the airport at 6:00 a.m. to fly to the next city in time to appear there on the 8:00 a.m. news. We developed a rather strange sleeping schedule: we would sleep from 1:00 a.m. to about 4:00 a.m., and after getting to the next town we would sleep until 3:00 or 4:00 p.m. Every once in a while we had a chance to rehearse.

Brazil was very unsafe at the time, and we often worried about the safety of our instruments. Once we even locked our instruments in a safe at the American Consulate in Rio de Janeiro. There were some interesting obstacles: the stage in a theater in Bogota, Columbia was raked at a 30-degree angle, so they put a block under the piano to keep the keyboard straight. Unfortunately there wasn't anything to do to compensate for my right hand being considerably higher than my left hand when I played the cello. We got our worst review of all time for that concert, and next day we learned that the American Embassy had been bombed.

After the days of unlimited mileage, touring became more expensive. When we went on tour to the Far East it cost $1,400 per person to get from Chicago to Singapore. I would have had to pay $1,400 for my cello to sit in the seat beside me, so instead I used my $1,400 for a travel case for my cello. It was made of steel, and my instrument was suspended inside it on straps and cushioned in foam rubber. The case weighed 50 pounds, which was far too heavy for me to carry. I solved the problem of getting from hotel to the concert hall without hurting myself by getting a canvas cello bag, which we stuffed with laundry. When we arrived at our hotel I took out the laundry, took the cello out of its steel case, and put it in the canvas case. Then I could get to concerts easily.

XVII. MAKING GOLD OUT OF TIN

Marek Janowski made his debut at the Lyric Opera with *Lohengrin* during the 1980 season. Once, at a reading rehearsal, Janowski took a good half hour to dress down the English horn player in front of the whole orchestra. I took that time to compose the response that I would make if he were to subject me to that sort of treatment: "Maestro, this is the best I can do, but it's not the worst I can do." I was able to use that statement four years later, when Janowski returned to conduct *Frau ohne Schatten*. He walked away from me after I said it, but he complimented me during the dress rehearsal. I told him that I hoped that my solo went as well on opening night, to which he responded, "Why wouldn't it?" I told him that I could get nervous, and he asked me why I would get nervous. I suppose that since conductors don't have to worry about playing in tune or playing difficult passages, they wouldn't have any reason to get nervous.

There's a cello solo in *Ariadne auf Naxos* that involves a large shift to a very high note on the A string, which I played with all due panache. Maestro Janowski asked me if I could play it without portamento, to which I responded, "Maestro, have you ever heard anyone play this solo without portamento and get the high G?" He told me that in Germany there are two who can do it. Then I ceremoniously played the solo without any kind of a slide, banging out the high G from six inches above the fingerboard, and said, "Now there are three cellists who can do it." I never took a shine to him, but Maestro Janowski seemed to take a real liking to me, and he congratulated me after many performances.

Jean Fournet (1913-2008) was a French flutist who had studied conducting with Philippe Gaubert. He began his conducting career in 1936, and became director of the Paris Opéra Comique and a professor of conducting at the École Normal de Musique in Paris in 1944. By the time he came to conduct at the Lyric Opera in 1965, the French style of interpreting opera had been pretty much a lost art. He revived it with his interpretations of works like Massenet's *Werther* and *Manon* and Debussy's *Palleas and Melisande.* Maestro Fournet was very severe and never smiled, which inspired some people in the orchestra to refer to him as "Stoneface" and "Mt. Rushmore."

There is an interlude between the fourth and fifth acts of Massenet's *Don Quichotte* that is for solo cello—a lesser-known parallel to the famous *Meditation from Thais* for solo violin. I had a great deal of respect for Fournet, so I played the solo in the Gaelic style, the way I imagined he would like it to be played (not the way I would usually play it). Fournet, who didn't speak English, came up to me at the end of the run and gave me a big hug and a kiss on both cheeks. Years later one of my colleagues approached Maestro Fournet when he conducted the Metropolitan Opera and told him that she was a friend of mine. His response was, "He is my friend."

I met Kenneth Schermerhorn on my very first American Ballet Theatre tour, and I worked with him on and off until he left the American Ballet Theatre in 1968. I was very glad when he returned in 1982 to conduct *Swan Lake*, because the demoralized, desensitized, and disinterested orchestra had not been sounding good for weeks. As soon as Maestro Schermerhorn started the overture, the members of the orchestra witnessed a dramatic change.

Maestro Schermerhorn delayed and elongated the second and fourth beats of the first several bars of the *Swan Lake* overture in a way that allowed the principal oboist enough time to fill the Metropolitan Opera House with his sound, and he supported the oboe solo with a heavier and more portentous accompaniment than we were accustomed to playing. By the time the overture ended we sounded like a first rate symphony orchestra.

Kenny's favorite quote was "If you can make a piece of garbage sound like great music, you are a real artist." He took great delight in finding the ultimate ways of phrasing tawdry music, and making it sound elegant. I shared his enthusiasm for using musical elasticity to figuratively make gold out of brass-colored tin.

Kenny left the American Ballet Theatre in 1968 to serve as the music director in Milwaukee, and came back to the ABT in 1982 in order, as he put it, "to put my girls through college." He moved on to become the Music Director of the Nashville Symphony, and stayed there for 20 years. He told me a few years before he died that he was happier there than he had ever been with his career and with his life. The feeling was obviously mutual since the Nashville Symphony named their hall in his honor.

In the early days of my time at the Lyric Opera, there was a lot of interaction between singers and instrumentalists, and certainly between singers and me. Geraint Evans was always happy to talk about his roles, particularly in *Wozzeck* and *Billy Budd*. Piero Cappuccilli and Martina Arroyo were very willing to go over the cello solos that acted as duets between the cello and singer in *Rigoletto* and *Masked Ball*, and would go through these duets as often as I needed to feel really comfortable with their rubatos.

Joan Sutherland came to the Lyric to sing the title role of *Lucia* in 1975. Her rendition of the famous "Mad Scene," was astonishing and compelling. I simply couldn't imagine how anybody could perform at that level, night after night. Since I had worked with Sutherland and her husband Richard Bonynge for several years I didn't consider it inappropriate to ask Bonynge if he would arrange for me to ask his wife a few questions in private. They invited me to come to their apartment at the Executive House on Wacker Drive before a performance of *Elektra*.

I decided to broach the subject of performing at such a high level night after night by complaining about my lazy cello section and how I had to do all the work. Joan Sutherland told me that when she started out at Covent Garden, she was probably a fifth-string Desdemona. Still, she was ready to walk out on the stage and deliver the role every night. She complained about how tired she was, and wondered whether she had five more years left in her (as it happened, she came back ten years later).

When I asked her how she did what she did, she told me that she first tried to sing everything perfectly in time and perfectly in tune, so that any liberty she might take was made from strength and not from weakness. She also told me that she spent most of her time relentlessly practicing the things that were really hard, and that she got a lot of help from Bonynge because of the way that he set things up. Bonynge was the only conductor I ever worked with who asked me to play as loud as I possibly could in a *bel canto* opera. When I mentioned that it was a first for me, he said, "What harm do you think you can do to the voices singing up there?" (one of which was Pavarotti).

I found him to be a very fine musician, particularly in the *bel canto* style, and deserved all of his success. I have a lovely autographed picture in my studio of Joan Sutherland thanking me for my most moving playing.

Another singer who was very generous to me was Placido Domingo. When he came to do *Lucia*, he sang the famous last aria half a tone down, which put us both in the key of D-flat major instead of the original key of D major. I protested and started to play the finale of *Don Quixote* in D-flat major. He told me that "*Don Quixote* is better in D major, but *Lucia* is better in D-flat major." He was right. The dying scene had much more pathos in D-flat than it did in the bright key of D major. Richard Tucker also sang this passage in D-flat major, but everybody else in my experience sang it in D major. After the first performance, Domingo insisted that I take a bow from the pit. I considered this extremely generous.

During the 1990s, I had the opportunity to work with some truly wonderful conductors at the Lyric Opera. The finest *Rosenkavalier* I ever played was with Jeri Kout, a Czechoslovakian conductor. He was probably the best conductor ever to step into the pit of the Lyric Opera, but he never achieved the great stardom that he deserved. His control over the orchestra was like Heifetz playing a violin concerto. Everybody vibrated at the same rate of speed. He achieved amazing nuances, particularly in an opera as difficult as *Rosenkavalier*. Maestro Kout had one encounter with Kathleen Battle who making a huge pain in the ass of herself while singing the role of Sophie. Kout finally called Ardis Krainik to the pit and said, "If the tantrums of a tempermental soprano are more important to you than a conductor who has done this work more than fifty times, you may keep your money and I will go back to Berlin tonight." Kathy was brought to heel. When Jeri Kout replaced Carlos Kleiber at the Metropolitan Opera for a performance of *Rosenkavalier*, they thought he was almost as good as Kleiber. Kleiber was considered God at the Met, so no higher compliment could ever be paid.

Another amazing experience was working with Zubin Mehta when he conducted Wagner's *Ring* in 1996. He stayed in the opera house practically around the clock, and was open to answering questions from anyone. He rehearsed us relentlessly, but he also showed appreciation for any real talent that he noticed in the orchestra. He brought out the best in us at all times.

At one point in *Das Rhinegold* there is a cello passage that was simply impossible to play at his tempo. I politely asked Mehta if he could tell me what cellists in other orchestras do with this passage, and he responded by saying, "If you don't know, who does?" I explained that the passage was simply too fast to be played, and he responded by saying, "That's no problem. I can gradually slow the tempo down for four bars, do the cello passage in a slower tempo, and then speed it up in another four bars." That's exactly what he did.

During another rehearsal when the first and second violins were not quite together, he described it as sort of like a horse race where one horse wins by a nose. After he repeated the passage, our principal violist said, "I think the nose is getting longer." When I repeated a passage one time too many in *Das Rheingold*, Mehta asked me "What would Leitner say?"

to which I replied, "He would give me a dirty look, and say, 'Vat are you doing?'"

Occasionally Mehta would do things that I felt were not respectful of the wishes of the composer, like pushing the tempo in the opening of *Sigfried* (he thought it was boring), but I loved his flexible approach to every other phrase in the *Ring*, and appreciated his strong connection to the musicians in the orchestra. Whenever I put a nice little slide in a solo, he would raise his eyebrows with pleasure. I will never forget his warm handshake after the first act of *Die Walkure* in the first Ring cycle, saying, "That was a *beautiful* solo."

I played *Masked Ball* and *Don Carlo* with Daniele Gatti. Gatti refused to accept my interpretation of the cello solo in the *Masked Ball*. He told me that it sounded too much like *Pagliacci*. He explained, "Here you have a situation with a woman whose husband believes she's committed adultery with his best friend, and in her heart she has. And he says, 'Now I'm going to kill you.' She pleads, 'Before you do, allow me to embrace my young son one more time.'" Gatti said to me, "Is this a cry or a whisper?" I told him, "You're a young man, but you have an old soul." When it came to *Don Carlo*, he explained to me that King Phillip was about 55 years old, and was too tired to try anymore. I explained that I was 55 and understood this man very well.

Christian Theilemann seemed to be on the sunny side of 40 when he conducted *Die Meistersinger* at the Lyric, and he embraced his German culture to a great degree. He seemed to almost be a reincarnation of Ferdinand Leitner, but with a much more flamboyant style. In the first intermission, he asked me whether I thought I could teach my colleagues to use the bow the way I did. I told him this was not going to happen for two reasons: the first was that my colleagues were not interested in learning anything from me, and the second was that it would take way more time than I had to do the job.

When I learned that my father had died right before the stage and orchestra rehearsals, Theilemann called me to offer his condolences and told me how terrible it was for him when his father died. Then he asked when I would come back to "help him." I did make it back for the first performance.

XVIII. THE DEATH OF LEONARD ROSE

I connected with Leonard Rose again in 1982 under circumstances that I unwittingly managed to arrange. My friend Dov Buk, an instrument dealer in New York, told me about an Amati cello that he was selling for Benar Heifetz. I told Dov that Leonard Rose had a Nicolo Amati cello, and when the two men met they became instant friends, who happened to have a lot in common.

Dov called me from his shop one day, and, as a kind of a prank, he put Leonard Rose on the phone without telling me who it was. After my initial annoyance, I had a pleasant conversation with Mr. Rose about instruments and how expensive it was for people like me to upgrade. I was, of course, not interested in upgrading, so when Mr. Rose asked me if I was a "looker," I replied that the business of looking was too rich for my blood.

He then told me about the physical frustrations of old age (he was 63 at the time). I let him know that the perfection of his solos in the recordings he made of the repertoire I knew so well, piano trios by Brahms, Schubert, Beethoven, and Mendelssohn, literally boggled my mind. His response was, "Every year it gets harder and harder, and so every year I practice longer and longer, but there is nothing else for me."

I asked him if he could recommend any former students for me to call to play in the cello section for the upcoming American Ballet Theater season. He recommended two cellists who became life-long friends: Eric Bartlett and Scott Ballantyne.

Eric was one of the founding members of the Orpheus Chamber Orchestra, and Scott, who taught at Juilliard and at the Cleveland Institute, knew the playing of the 12-year-old Matt Haimowitz, a cellist Leonard Rose claimed would be the next Yo-Yo Ma. Scott told me that he was very good. I asked Scott if Matt played better than I played, to which he responded, "He plays better than you did when you were twelve." Eric played principal during my leaves of absence in 1994 and 1996, and John Lanchbery sent me a letter letting me know that my section was in "talented and capable hands." Scott and Eric continued playing in my section until I left in 1998, and both have moved on to further successes. Eric is a member of the New York Philharmonic, and Scott has a great career as a teacher, soloist, and chamber musician.

Leonard Rose was diagnosed with leukemia in 1984. I heard him give a beautiful and inspiring performance of the Schumann Concerto with the Israeli Chamber Orchestra in January of that year. Somehow musical impulse triumphed over his many physical difficulties. When I saw him backstage, he told me that he knew what tired was, but that this was something quite different.

I asked Scott Ballantyne, Mr. Rose's former student and very close assistant, if he could arrange for me to see Mr. Rose during the final days of his illness (and his life). Mr. Rose's response was that he didn't want me to see him, and certainly didn't want me to come to his funeral or "any damned fool memorial service they may concoct for me at Juilliard." He said that what he wanted me to do was to "play glorious solos in the opera."

The evening of the day he died was the opening night of Strauss' *Die Frau ohne Schatten*, an opera with the biggest and most exposed cello solos in the repertoire. I tried to imagine how I could possibly play it in a way that would be good enough to honor Leonard Rose. Ironically the next time this opera came to the Lyric, opening night was on the 23rd anniversary of his death.

XIX. AN INEVITABLE SENSE OF RUBATO

I resigned from the American Ballet Theatre orchestra in 1998 after June and I decided to relocate permanently to Chicago. Our building, like other buildings all over New York's Upper West Side, became a condominium, and we were faced with buying it or buying a much nicer apartment in Chicago, where we spent much of the year anyway. I took Bert Lucerelli's advice to develop my career in New York when I joined the Lyric Opera, and by 1998 I was happy to take what I had built, and hone it in the comfort of a spacious apartment on Lake Shore Drive with a view of Lake Michigan. I also learned to drive, something I never could have imagined doing in New York.

Eric Larsen, who had become a senior member of the faculty at the North Carolina School of the Arts, could fly as easily to Chicago as he could fly to New York for rehearsals, so we were able to work on repertoire we would perform and record.

Eric and I are of much the same mind when it comes to practicing and rehearsing, and we developed ways to maximize our time. First we would work through the piano part, using the moving lines in the left hand of the piano as our guide, until we had the phrasing and timing exactly the way we wanted it. Then we would work for what I like to call "composite sound," trying to reconcile the tonal disparity between the piano and the cello. Then we would spend the rest of our rehearsal time working at very slow tempos with the metronome, gradually increasing it until we reached our ultimate performance tempo.

When rehearsing with the trio, we would work phrase by phrase to try to combine inevitability with a sense of rubato. We never compromised, and worked on phrases until we agreed exactly what we would do with them together. We delighted in good phrases, and worked for them endlessly. Sometimes we experimented. I remember once during our 1981 tour, we tried to see how far we could exaggerate a phrase and still have it make sense. Thirty years later I think we could have gone further. I'm proud of the recordings we made together, particularly the Chopin Introduction and Polonaise, the Rachmaninoff Sonata, the two early Beethoven Sonatas, the Brahms F Major Sonata, the Archduke Trio, the Brahms B Major Trio and the Ravel Trio. I also like the video we made of the Shostakovich Trio; it shows a lot of what we tried to accomplish.

During the 1960s through the 1980s it was expensive and difficult to produce long-playing vinyl records. CDs were much easier to produce, but without distribution those recordings didn't have credibility. My dear friend Henson Markham and his brother had a record-producing factory, and though most of their recordings were of Country and Western music, it didn't prevent them from producing runs of 1,000 of my CDs at a very reasonable price.

Internet-based commerce made it possible for me to have a recording career. It entirely eliminated the problem of having a distributor. While there are certainly down sides to the changes in the way people buy recordings, initially this freedom from a distributor leveled the playing field, and made it possible for someone like me to be credible as a recording artist based on my credibility as a musician.

I feel extremely fortunate to have Leonard Rose as a constant source of inspiration. Many of the great virtuoso cellists of the past are remembered for their particular personalities and some are remembered for the way they have contributed to the virtuoso possibilities for the cello. Leonard Rose certainly had a formidable personality, but he will mainly be remembered for his perfect intonation, beautiful sound, elegant phrasing, and the emotional warmth he put into playing every note. His integrity and intelligence were matchless.

He tried to get his students to aspire to the standards and qualities he aspired to, and achieved success by not allowing students to play pieces that were too difficult for them to play at their highest level. I remember being resentful when Mr. Rose insisted that I play the Saint-Saëns Concerto for my jury at Juilliard instead of the Dvořák Concerto. He knew that I could play the Saint-Saëns Concerto well, and he knew that the Dvořák Concerto would have been a struggle for me to play well. Understanding the importance of making a good impression was one of the gifts that he gave to me. His philosophy was to spend half one's practice time developing and maintaining technical skills with scales, exercises, and etudes, and to always keep practicing and performing technically difficult pieces, so that everything else you might be asked to play would seem easy by comparison. I try to give as much of what I learned from Leonard Rose to my students.

I use what I have learned to teach my students to sound as good as they can, any way they can. If something doesn't sound good, it doesn't sound good in particular ways: there could be problems with intonation, rhythm, or sound quality. There's always a correlation between what I hear when a student plays and the physical means the student uses to produce what I hear. I spot the problem, define it, and then I come up with some sort of an exercise to bridge the gap between where the student is technically and what will make him or her consistently sound better. First I consider why something is happening and what can be changed to produce a better result. I believe that there isn't any mystery to sounding good, and believe that sounding good is, obviously, always better than sounding bad. Many people don't seem to see this, but that's their problem.

During the 1980s I had a reputation for being able to help cellists sound good when playing under pressure, so young professionals, many who were graduates of the Juilliard, Manhattan, and Yale music schools, would come to me for lessons. I had the good fortune to play thousands of solos in big opera houses, and those solos gave me a laboratory in which to experiment. It has been a great privilege to be able to pass on some of the knowledge I learned from my experiments to some of my professional colleagues.

The clarinetist Jon Manasse played for me before taking his audition for principal clarinet position of the Metropolitan Opera. When he played the famous solo from the second act of *La Traviata*, I clapped out the subdivisions. This gave his playing a poignancy that wasn't there before, and he immediately told me, "What you just taught me means that I can control the destiny of every phrase I play for the rest of my life." He won the audition, and he tells me that what I taught him about subdivision is one of the main things that he teaches his Juilliard and Eastman students.

James Kreger, a fantastic cellist, came to play for me in preparation for a Metropolitan Opera audition. Everything sounded good, except for a fast-moving excerpt in Verdi's Aida, which he simply could not play at the required tempo. I broke the excerpt into sequential units with breaks in between, and he was immediately able to play the passage at breakneck speed. What held him back was the constant connecting of the end of one sequence to the beginning of the next. When he could picture this excerpt as a series of units of release, the obstacles that he created for himself vanished. He won the audition.

Patrick Jee joined the Chicago Lyric Opera as my assistant a year before he was scheduled to play a performance of the Tchaikovsky "Rococo" Variations with the Moscow Chamber Orchestra. During the intermissions I showed him the detaché bowing as it had been shown to me by Leonard Rose. He gave an excellent performance, and told me that the Rose detaché made a huge difference in his rendition of the final variation.

Eliot Bailen was one of the greatest talents who ever crossed my path. He worked with me for many years, but I can't remember what I taught him. I suppose I was able to help him amplify his sound and get a little more bite into his bow arm, but in all fairness, from his first lesson, when he played the big solo from Strauss' *Bourgeois Gentilhomme*, I felt that I should be paying him for the beauty and pleasure he brought into my life with his wonderful talent.

I was able to give him useful professional advice, though. Eliot felt that he had to prove himself to every cellist in sight in order to feel legitimate. I kept telling him that every other cellist was his rival, and they didn't want to be illuminated. I explained to him that working his way through the ranks was simply not the way to go. After ten years of nagging, I finally got him to give a New York recital in a major hall. It was a stunning event. At the end of the recital, he told me, "Now that I'm on the other side of it, I know why you wanted me to do it." Reviews of cello recitals by Lynn Harrell, Yo-Yo Ma, Janos Starker, and Eliot Bailen that were played in New York came out in the next month's issue of *Strings* Magazine. Eliot got the best review, by far. He has since enjoyed great success as a member of the faculty of Columbia University, directing and performing in several chamber music societies, and writing music of real significance.

My Lyric Opera colleague Walter Preucil had never studied with Leonard Rose, but I was able to bring him into Leonard Rose's world technically, tonally, and musically. At the time of this writing, he is playing principal cello at the Lyric Opera, and sitting in my old chair.

Barbara Bogatin, one of my stand partners at the American Ballet Theatre, came to me before playing an audition for the assistant principal chair in the New York Philharmonic. She was having trouble with intonation in Strauss' *Also Sprach Zarathustra*. I had her play each first note of each group of four sixteenth notes four times. I had her do this through chromatic passages, until she could hear recognizable varieties of seventh chords emerge. Once she recognized that outline, she played the excerpt perfectly in tune. She didn't win the audition, but Zubin Mehta did listen to her play for an hour. She served as the principal cellist of the New Jersey and Milwaukee symphonies, and then joined the San Francisco Symphony.

Rosalyn Clarke had trouble vibrating on her third finger. We tried strengthening exercises, but eventually I suggested that she should forget about trying to vibrate on that finger and simply try to get the most beautiful sound she could without vibrato. In a very short time she was vibrating on that third finger perfectly well. Once she had a long cello solo in Haydn's Mass in Time of War, and was particularly concerned about it because the performance was going to be broadcast on the radio. Her sound was constricted when she played it for me a few hours before the performance.

The solo was in the key of A major, so I had Lindy (as she is called) play some three-octave A major scales, using one bow per scale degree. I had her hold each note for two beats, while the metronome clicked half notes at 60 beats per minute. Then I accompanied her with a stream of double stops that created a series of dominant seventh chords. After 25 minutes she sounded great. She has been the assistant principal at the Orchestra of St. Luke's for the last 30-odd years, and has had a very successful career as a freelancer in New York.

Joseph Kimura was a very gifted student, but he suffered from intonation problems. He had particular trouble with augmented 4ths and minor 6ths. I asked him to play the first three notes of "Maria" from Leonard Bernstein's West Side Story (the first two notes outline an augmented 4th), and to my amazement, he played it perfectly in tune. I sent him home with instructions to find twelve tunes, one for each possible interval. From then on, every time he played out of tune, I would have him play the appropriate tune for that particular interval and then repeat the passage as written. The improvement was dramatic and within a few weeks, he no longer needed to refer to his interval list to maintain his newly acquired sense of pitch.

I have also taught many students who didn't play very well at first, but made enough progress with me to become successful. Seth Woods was a student at Roosevelt University who had severe intonation problems. He came to me after being told that if he didn't improve he would lose his scholarship. His problem was that he didn't know where the notes he was trying to play actually were on the cello. I put him on a steady diet of scale exercises, and after a year and a half, he was able to play the Shostakovich Sonata and the Boccherini Concerto well enough to get a large scholarship at Brooklyn College. He studied there with Frederick Zlotkin, the principal cellist of the New York City Ballet, and after a year, he got a scholarship to study in Switzerland with Thomas Demenga and has become well known in eclectic new music circles.

EPILOGUE

The musical world that I knew when I was growing up was very different from the musical world we have today. When I was a student at Midwood High School in Brooklyn and principal cellist of the All City High School Orchestra, I was selected to present Van Cliburn with an award from the music students of New York at a ticker-tape parade held in his honor after he won the first Tchaikovsky Piano Competition. As we were being photographed for the centerfold of the New York Daily News, he said, "I hope that my victory will help the next generation have an easier time making a career." For awhile, this generated a lot of interest in competitions, but no careers on the Van Cliburn scale were launched.

I heard Mstislav Rostropovich give his New York debut recital at Carnegie Hall, and I had the opportunity to hear David Oistrakh, Nathan Milstein, and Leonard Rose play concerts there as well. I aspired to be like them. They inspired and motivated me to play the best I could under every circumstance through my entire career, and enriched my life in every possible way. It seemed possible, if you did the right things, you would have the right outcomes, as I believe I did in my career.

In the musical world of my youth a fairly large number of big names dominated the field. Most of their names are still recognized: Rubinstein, Horowitz, Heifetz, Rostropovich, Oistrakh, Gilels, Bernstein, von Karajan, and others. There were also a great many exceptional musicians around who were appreciated by large audiences, and a considerable number of musicians who, though they did not have substantial solo careers were, nevertheless, able to support themselves as musicians. Now everything seems to work in reverse. Thanks to a generation of excellent teachers, there seem to be more capable musicians around than there are audiences to support them, and child prodigies are nearly a dime a dozen. The possibilities of gainful professional employment for young musicians who play traditional repertoire are slim.

I feel very fortunate to have lived through an era where, by taking my destiny into my own hands, I was able to have a truly fulfilling career in music. It is possible that such an era will return, but in the meantime it is vital to continue passing on the love of music to future generations, regardless whether seeking it produces gainful employment. Living a musical life is to spend time in the company of greatness.

ABOUT THE AUTHOR

Praised as a "first-rate cellist" in *The New York Times* and a "superb cellist" in *The Strad*, Daniel Morganstern has presented most of the standard repertoire in his New York recitals that have included three at Alice Tully Hall in Lincoln Center, five at Carnegie Recital Hall, and others at the Lincoln Center Library and the New York Cultural Center. He served as Principal Cellist for the Lyric Opera of Chicago and the American Ballet Theatre at the Metropolitan Opera House for over 40 years. His recordings include sonatas by Chopin, Brahms, Schubert, Beethoven (complete), and Rachmaninoff; trios by Brahms (complete), Beethoven, Ravel, and Tchaikovsky; and duos by Ravel and Kodály. His editions for International Music Company include concertos by Dvořák, Schumann, Saint-Saëns, Boccherini, Elgar, and Tchaikovsky; the cello parts to three Brahms trios; *Fundamentals of Cello Technique*; *Cello Solos from Opera and Ballet*; and a transcription of the Schumann A Minor Violin Sonata. His treatise *Practice for Performance* is published by Mel Bay, and his articles appear in *The Instrumentalist*. He has been on the faculty of the Aspen Music School, the String Academy at Indiana University, and the Meadowmount School of Music.

28323201R00057

Made in the USA
Charleston, SC
07 April 2014